So Far Away in the World

Stories from the Swedish Twin Cities

Anne Gillespie Lewis

NODIN PRESS

ISBN: 0-931714-94-X

Library of Congress Control Number: 2001097765
First Edition

Nodin Press, a division of Micawber's, Inc.
525 North Third Street
Minneapolis, MN 55401

Dedicated to the memory of Phyllis Johnson Elfstrom,
who loved a country she never saw

Contents

Foreword ix

Acknowledgments xi

Chapter One—Just Another Swede Town 13

    I think I'm Sweden 13

    Just another Swede town 13

    Grace Blomquist Anderson

        Are you winking at me, Grace? 18

    Charlotte Lindquist Hansen

        One of the Lindquist kids 23

    Phyllis Johnson Elfstrom

        Her heart was in Värmland 27

Chapter Two—So Far Away in the World 33

    Bertha Brunius

        A light heart on the frontier 33

    Albin E. Johnson

        An immigrant's paper trail 36

    John P. Wallberg

        "Next Christmas I'll be home" 43

Chapter Three—The New Newcomers 47

    Ewa and Anders Rydåker

        Living in two worlds 47

    Mariann Tiblin

        Minneapolis resident, citizen of the world 52

    Margareta Jern Beyer and Bill Beyer

        Balancing two cultures 55

Chapter Four—Swedes at Work 59

    Annie Robertson

        "All rests with Annie the cook" 59

    Annie the cook, Lizzie the nursemaid

        and thousands of others 65

    Axel Ohman

        He built half of Minneapolis 69

    Victor Fridlund

        A visit with Uncle Vic 73

    Axel Johnson

        Keeper of the White Star 79

Chapter Five—Swedes at Play 83

    Saturday night fever—Swedish style 83

    Cliff Brunzell

        The man with the golden strings 83

    The life and times of the Corona Band 91

    Gunhild Karlsson Anderson

        The girl who loved to dance 93

    Lorraine Wallberg McGrath

        Spinn, spinn, spinn, dottern min 102

    Don Carlson

        The original Laker 107

Chapter Six—Body and Soul   **111**

Audrey Grann Johnson
  Swedes in stripes   111
Mildred Soderholm Grann
  A peek in Sody's diary   114
A church-going people   117
Eric Norelius
  A young man and his blind horse   118
William Hyllengren
  Still serving his master   121
Ten little Youngdahls and how they grew   124
Mount Olivet
  The church that Reuben built   127

Chapter Seven—The Next Generations   **129**

Renee Weberg Gillespie
  A little girl just like grandma   129
Gretchen Carlson
  Growing up Swedish   132
Barbara Flanagan Sanford
  Another secret Swede   133
Wendell Anderson
  From the east side to the king's side   136

Chapter Eight—For a Swedish Accent   **139**

Nu är det jul igen   139
The great Swedish sausage war   143
Ingebretsen's
  Need we say more?   146
The American Swedish Institute
  Swedish culture and coffee, too   149
Swan J. Turnblad
  A son of Småland makes it big   153
Bruce Karstadt
  On the state of Swedishness   156

Epilogue   **159**

Not for Swedes Only   **161**

Endnotes   **163**

Bibliography   **167**

Permissions   **169**

Recipe Index   **171**

Index   **172**

Foreword

Swedish immigrants began to settle in the early 1850s in the small towns of St. Paul and Minneapolis along the Mississippi River in the Minnesota Territory. By 1905, over 126,000 Swedes lived in Minnesota, almost one-third (38,000) residing in the Twin Cities. Fifteen years later, the Swedish-born population was still the largest immigrant group in both Minneapolis and St. Paul. In 1990, a little more than 100,000 people in the Twin Cities identified themselves as being of Swedish heritage. Yet today, immigrants from Sweden continue to arrive, settle and make a life for themselves in Minneapolis and St. Paul.

A 1996 conference on Swedish life in the Twin Cities brought to the forefront just how important a role Swedish immigrants and their descendants played in helping to develop these two great cities. Philip Anderson and Dag Blanck, editors of the recent publication *Swedes in the Twin Cities,* have observed that "it can safely be argued that the Twin Cities is the metropolitan area that today exhibits the highest degree of Swedish-American visibility or consciousness, where a sense of Swedishness still prevails."

In this collection of marvelously written stories, Anne Gillespie Lewis makes an important contribution to understanding a fuller picture of the Swedish-American community in the Twin Cities, past and present. These stories, written with such poignancy and humor, are wonderfully descriptive of the people who make up this community.

Through these personal narratives, she draws us into many different aspects of the lives of Swedish-Americans in the Twin Cities that to date have largely been unexplored. We are taken from Inga Svensson the cook at the Ramsey House to Pete Peterson's popcorn wagon at Camden Park to Saturday night fever "Swedish style" in the forty or more dance halls alongside Cedar Avenue. She explores with equal affection the experiences of immigrants in the early 1900s and those of the twenty-first century.

I want to thank Anne Gillespie Lewis for capturing the memories, the sounds, sometimes even the smell and taste of the lives of Swedes in Minneapolis and St. Paul. Enjoy it!

Bruce Karstadt
Executive Director
The American Swedish Institute

Acknowledgments

Many people have helped with the writing of this book, which began with a casual meeting with Norton Stillman, publisher of Nodin Press, who asked me if I would be interested in writing it. A big "thank you for asking" to him and *"tack så mycket"* to Marita Karlisch, archivist at the American Swedish Institute, for her enthusiasm, interest, and generous help, and to my friend Ewa Rydåker, who gave so generously of her suggestions, time and coffee! Jan McElfish, at the American Swedish Institute, was very helpful in making suggestions and giving encouragement. Thanks also to Norton Stillman's assistant, Ardie Eckardt, who was ever cheerful and willing to answer questions as the book took shape. Deb Miller and other staff members of the Minnesota Historical Society, staff at the Minneapolis Collection of the Minneapolis Public Library and Micki Cook at the Carver County Historical Society were very helpful. Dana Heimark at the Alexander Ramsey House in St. Paul patiently looked through the Ramsey papers to provide quotes about Annie Robertson.

I am grateful to the people who allowed me to interview them for the book, gave me their favorite recipes and loaned their precious photos for scanning. Thanks, also, to those who so kindly read portions of the manuscript. They are, in random order, my brother Mike Gillespie, Bob Johnson, Ewa and Anders Rydåker, the Hon. Wendell Anderson, Prof. Teddy Brunius, Cliff Brunzell, Pixie Elfstrom Haug, Lauri Elfstrom Bassett, Marci Elfstrom Osborne, Kim Elfstrom Johnson, Jan McElfish, Axel and Goody Ohman, the late Gunhild Anderson, Inger Pignolet, Marilyn Brakke, Lorraine McGrath, Mariann Tiblin, Ann-Christine Moonen, Barbara Flanagan Sanford, Pastor William Hyllengren, Pastor Jim Anderson, Mike Haeuser, Opal Ronning, Dave Carlson, Julie Ingebretsen, Vic and Lindy Fridlund, Polly Thill, Jean Johnson, Audrey Johnson, Lois and Charlie Anderson, Bruce Karstadt, Dana Heimark, Carole Neumann, Charlotte Lindquist Hansen, Margareta Beyer, Lawrence Hammerstrom, Helene Carlson, Renee Gillespie, Gretchen Carlson, Ardis Anderson, Jean Ross, and last, but far from least, my helpful and patient husband, Stephen Lewis.

There are too many tales of Swedes in the Twin Cities to fit into one book. I know I have missed many good stories, but I hope we will continue to tell them to each other and to our children.

Four clerks posed outside Charles Blomquist's grocery store in Camden in north Minneapolis. They are, left to right, Magnus (Mike) Anderson, unidentified, Ben Nelson and John Chriss. Photo courtesy of Minneapolis Public Library, Minneapolis Collection.

Chapter One

Just Another Swede Town

I think I'm Sweden

What's a person with a name like mine doing writing a book on Swedes in the Twin Cities? Let me tell you a family story. My brother Mike (John Michael Gillespie, named for our dad) was in kindergarten at Hamilton School in north Minneapolis years ago when his teacher asked the kids in the class what nationality they were. When she came to Mike, as she related to my mother, "Here's this child who looks Italian, has a name as Irish as Paddy's pig and he says to me, 'I don't know but I think I'm Sweden.'" He was right, we are "Sweden" (and Norwegian and Irish), just two of the thousands of people living in the Twin City area who claim at least a bit of Swedish heritage. Not all of us have names like Johnson, Olson or Carlson—though I must say our mother's name was Anderson. Not all of us are tall and blonde. We may not all spend any time thinking about or celebrating our Swedish heritage—though some Swedish-Americans work hard to keep up traditions—but all of us come from families that have gone "So Far Away in the World."

Just another Swede town

I grew up in Camden, on the far north side of Minneapolis, close enough to the west bank of the Mississippi River so that many of us got bats in our houses in summer—at least we blamed the bats on our nearness to the river. Camden was one of the many "Swede towns" in Minneapolis and St. Paul. It was among the earliest areas to draw immigrants from Sweden. In fact, except for the Cedar-Riverside area, what was then Ward 10—Camden—had the highest percent of Swedish-born residents in Minneapolis in 1905, according to John Rice, writing in *They Chose Minnesota: A Survey of the State's Ethnic Groups.*[1]

Swede Hollow, on the east side of St. Paul, was the oldest enclave of Swedish immigrants. Today the hollow is a green glade, with a sweeping view of downtown St. Paul from the top of its rim. Below, where there were haphazard clusters of houses—some not more than shacks—the silver sliver of Phalen Creek runs through the ravine and the signs of the lively community of immigrants are nearly impossible to detect. The Swedes came and went over a couple of decades, in the late nineteenth century. They were followed by waves of other immigrants and worsening sanitary conditions in the hollow and eventually the city of St. Paul stepped in, condemned the whole hollow and tore all the houses down. By that time, of course, the Swedes were long gone.

In Minneapolis, the first pockets of Swedish settlement were along Washington and Cedar Avenues, in the

The Nelson family ran this boarding house at 4301 Lyndale Avenue North. Mr. Nelson, second from right, was a streetcar conductor. Photo courtesy of the Minneapolis Public Library, Minneapolis Collection.

area still known as Seven Corners, although a couple of corners have been cut—quite literally—as the city grew and redeveloped. The Swedes spread south and southwest. They also went north, drawn to the Camden area by work. A Swedish immigrant with the unlikely name of C. A. Smith had a sawmill there that drew many immigrant workers.

The men who worked for the mill often lived in the many big old boarding houses in the Camden area. One of these, a large, white frame house with a spectacular porch running across its front, was run by Christine Nelson. Her granddaughter, Arlett Bredesen Nelson, told me that all the children in her mother's family had

to help. "When my mother was little, she had to stand on a stool to wash the dishes," Arlett said.

When I was growing up, the Swedish presence was still felt in Camden, but lightly. We thought it was normal that many of our friends and nearly all the merchants in the shopping area a few blocks away had Swedish or Norwegian names. There was John Nelson the shoe repair man, Johnson Drug on the corner of Lyndale and 42nd, Herman Johnson the tailor and his partner, Berg, and Blomquist the grocer. Up on 42nd and Fremont were Carl Nelson, another grocer, Al Anderson, who had the gas station, and the Falk drug store, later owned by another Swede, Don Carlson.

There was a rivalry between the ethnic groups who lived in Camden, particularly the Swedes and Norwegians. My friend Ardis Krefting Anderson, whose father's family were early Camden residents, told me her dad used to quote a little rhyme that the Norwegians used to tease the Swedish kids. It was:

Swedie, Swedie,
stuck on straw,
can't say nuthin'
but ya, ya, ya!

By the time I was a kid, there was no Swedish to be heard on the street, although many of the oldtimers and some of their children could still speak the language. Salem Evangelical Lutheran Church, on 42nd and Dupont, was the oldest Swedish Lutheran church in Camden. Before my time, there were dance halls and boarding houses and other signs of the immigrant life.

But the Swedes didn't disappear, they just blended more and more into the American fabric. On our block, bounded by Webber Parkway, 43rd Avenue, and Dupont and Emerson Avenues, the roll call of Swedes or part-Swedes is impressive. We ourselves were a little bit Swedish, the Elfstroms were more than half and their mom, Phyllis Johnson Elfstrom, was all Swedish. Next to them were Opal and Jim Ronning, a couple of lovable Norwegians. Up a few houses was Harry Johnson, Phyllis' cousin, another Swede. The Storms were part Scandinavian, I think. The Leverentz family was half Swede, Ronnie Lorentzen was another Swedish-Norwegian combination, and I guess the Swedlunds were Swedes, too. Al Anderson—the gas station guy—probably was another one.

This photo of my brother Mike (John M. Gillespie, Jr.) and me was taken by our dad, John M. Gillespie, Sr, in our back yard. Photo courtesy of Anne Gillespie Lewis.

The pool at Camden Park was always busy on summer days. This photo was taken in 1954. See anyone you know? The author thinks she is at the right, in the foreground, behind a girl with her right hand in the air. Photo courtesy of the Minneapolis Public Library, Minneapolis Collection.

Across the street, Leslie and Jimmy Shaft were half Scandinavian and half Polish. They lived in an extended family—with their mom and dad and aunt and grandma. Their dad, Big Jim, worked at the water works just across the Camden bridge. Their mom, Shirley Bjerk Shaft and her sister, Evie Bjerk, and their grandmother, Nellie Bjerk, were Swedes, too. Nellie, a little bit of a thing, was born on the boat coming over from Sweden. The family even had a dog—a beagle who was terrified of thunderstorms—with a Swedish name, *flicka*. Next to the Shafts were the Nielands. Russ Nieland was part of our gang and his mom was Swedish. He even knows where the Swedish side is from—Jämtland, up in the north of Sweden.

We neighborhood kids spent our summers in the pool at Camden Park [officially called Webber Park, but we never called it that], right across the street from my house. A low barrier, made of rough concrete that regularly scraped the knees of unwary kids, separated the shallow pool from the deeper end. After we were done swimming, if we had a nickel, we would line up at the popcorn wagon. Pete Peterson—at least I guess that was his name—painted slogans on his old popcorn truck. The one every old Camden kid remembers is "Smile and the world smiles with you, crab and you crab alone."

In winter, we skated on the pond in Camden Park for hours on end. Saturday afternoons we trooped to the Camden Theatre for our weekly fix of cowboy and Zorro movies. Years later, when I heard Linda Ronstadt's album of Mexican music, I wondered why it sounded so familiar; then I realized that the melodies were background music to the Zorro films.

We played outdoors after supper when the weather permitted. Television was in its infancy, at least in our neighborhood, so the old-fashioned games—"Pom Pom Pullaway," "Red Rover," "Old Lady Witch," and "Statues"—were among our favorites. In summer, we played baseball. I should say, the rest of them played baseball and I tried to stay in the outfield and hoped nobody would hit one my way. On a couple of occasions, Shirley Shaft joined the game and she could hit them right in the lake!

The Camden area is vastly changed since I grew up in the 1950s and early sixties. The shopping strip on the northwest corner of the intersection of 42nd and Lyndale has been torn down and a Subway sandwich shop and the sprawling new home of the doctors' group I have been going to for more than fifty years— Camden Physicians— replaced the old buildings. So now, instead of going to the Camden Theatre to watch cowboy movies at the Saturday matinees, I go to the same space to have my doctor check my blood pressure. Of course, even in my day, Camden was far different from the Camden of Grace Blomquist Anderson or Charlotte Lindquist Hansen, who grew up earlier in the twentieth century on the other side of the railroad tracks from Camden Park. Grace's and Charlotte's stories are included in this chapter. Here, too, is the story of Phyllis Johnson Elfstrom, another Camden Swede, and, oh, how I wish she were still here to read it.

Grace Blomquist Anderson, with her parents Elin and Charles Blomquist. Petri and Svenson photo, courtesy of Charles and Lois Anderson.

Grace Blomquist Anderson
Are you winking at me, Grace?

When I was a little girl, my mother shopped for groceries at Blomquist's Red and White Grocery in Camden. I loved going to Blomquist's with my mom to order the groceries—which were later delivered to our house by Grace's son Charlie—and the reason I loved it

was Grace. Her name was Grace Anderson, but many people still called her by her maiden name, Grace Blomquist. Grace had a merry way about her and she must have loved little children. I think I remember sitting on the counter. I think I remember Grace giving me a piece of candy. I even think I remember Grace winking at me. I loved Grace.

Grace and her husband Malcolm and Grace's brother, Vernon, took over the store when their dad, Charlie, died in 1947. They ran it until sometime in the fifties and then closed it. After that, we went up to 42nd and Fremont to shop. Once in a while, my mother would talk about the Blomquists and wonder what they were up to. My memories of Grace faded, but I had fleeting thoughts of her, and mentions of the Blomquists always summoned up happy, hazy memories.

Grace lived to be 95 years old and died only ten months ago, still alert to the last. What's more, she had followed my off-and-on career as a newspaper reporter for years and was very proud of me, according to her daughter-in-law Lois Anderson. I felt enormously pleased, very touched, and awfully sad. Here Grace was winking at me all those years and I didn't know it.

Her son talked about his mom when I went to visit him and Lois in their house on Victory Avenue in north Minneapolis. Charlie Anderson's a big guy. When he played football for Minneapolis Henry High School, he weighed close to 300 pounds. He looked familiar to me when he opened the door, though I hadn't seen him in nearly fifty years. His wife, Lois, is a pretty woman with small bones and quick movements. Both are mightily interested in genealogy and even give talks on it to groups. A lot of people in Minneapolis say they're Swedish, but Charlie takes it one step further. He says he's three-fourths *Värmlänning* and the other quarter is from Småland. The Blomquists came from Småland.

So they knew all about the Blomquists. They knew that Charlie Anderson's great-grandfathers, Peter Öst- lund and Franz Nicholson, were early settlers in Camden. Before Franz came to the little community, however, he and some buddies from Sweden worked up in the woods. They had a picture taken, all in suits rented from the photographer, Lois said. "Franz and his son, Charlie, came to Red Wing in 1881 and they went right up to Taylor's Falls to work; the women followed in 1882," said Lois. The family lived in Franconia and in Shafer, Minnesota, before they settled in Camden in 1884. Franz came from Småland, one of the poorest provinces in Sweden. His name changed along the way and his son was known as Charlie Blomquist, though his given name was Carl.

In those days, men took whatever job they could find and Franz found one hauling bricks at the brickyard on north Lyndale with a team of horses. Either Franz or his son could have had the job, but Charlie let his dad take it. Franz was working with his team of horses on Christmas Eve when he was hit by a streetcar and killed. Sadly, his son was on that very streetcar. Charlie's mother kept the family together somehow.

Charlie Blomquist married Peter Östlund's daugh- ter. Elin. Peter Östlund worked for the Compo-Board factory on 45th and Lyndale, running the elevator. "The building is still there, you can see the name on it," said Charlie Anderson. "Sometimes he'd get laid off and then he and my Aunt Minnie would walk up the hill to Crystal Lake Cemetery and he'd lay flowers on the grave of his wife. I remember walking up there with him."

Franz Nicholson and his son, Charlie Blomquist, both worked as lumberjacks when they first came to Minne- sota. The family says that the 'jacks rented the suits from the photographer for the picture. Franz is at left, in back, and Charlie is at right, also in the back row. Photo courtesy of Charles and Lois Anderson.

Charlie Blomquist is pictured in his store at 4211 Webber Parkway in Camden in 1913. Note the Christmas decorations on the ceiling. Photo courtesy of Charles and Lois Anderson.

Charlie Blomquist got into the grocery business first on 46th and Lyndale, where he employed a young man named Harry Lindquist, whose daughter's story is also in this chapter. Later, Charlie opened the store at 4211 Webber Parkway, in the heart of the Camden business district. "I think he did pretty well; he had a number of clerks working for him," said Charlie Anderson.

Grace interviewed Harry Lindquist when he was in his nineties. Harry said her dad employed seven or eight men and served both the Camden area and the nearby suburb of Brooklyn Center. At first, before they had trucks, they kept horses in a barn behind the store. Harry said they used to go to the market at 5 a.m. to buy produce.

Blomquist's was noted for fresh produce, crock butter and cheese aged on the premises.

Charlie Blomquist, Harry said, was a kind man, who never bawled him out and was the best boss he ever had. Charlie paid him eight dollars a week when he started.

The Blomquists lived close to the store, on 46th Avenue between Camden and Aldrich Avenues. There, on October 29, 1904, Grace Audrey Louise Blomquist was born. When she was four years old, her family moved to 4601 Camden. The house remained in the family until 1976. Grace went to Hamilton School, just as I did many years later, and she played down by the river, something I was strictly forbidden to do. When

Grace was a child, logging was king and the Mississippi was almost solid with logs floating downstream. The temptation was too much for Grace and her friends. I wonder if her mother knew that she often scrambled across the river over the tops of the logs? "She got pretty good at it," said her son.

Charlie Blomquist was born in Sweden, but he wouldn't allow Swedish to be spoken in his home. "I only heard him speak Swedish once," said Charlie Anderson. Some woman came in to the store and accused him of selling her broken eggs. "He let her have it in Swedish. Told her never to come in his store again."

Despite the ban on Swedish at home, Grace took it at North High School and learned it well. She enjoyed speaking it with relatives and visitors from Sweden all her life. She and her husband, Malcolm, who also spoke Swedish, even sang Swedish hymns on his brother-in-law's radio show. Grace went to Sweden once, on a tour. She didn't look up the old family homesteads, however. "I guess she got that from her dad," said her son. "He figured 'We've left Sweden now. We're in America.'"

Like many women of her age group, Grace worked at the Twin Cities Arsenal, making ammunition, during World War II. By that time, she was long married and the mother of two children, Charlie—actually Malcolm Charles, who never went by the name "Malcolm," and Natalie. After the store closed, Charlie Anderson said, Grace worked at Pillsbury for ten years taking care of the expense accounts before she finally retired.

All through her many years, Salem Lutheran Church played a big part in her life. Her dad was one of the founders of the church in 1895. He was the one, of all the Swedes, who went down to the Augustana Synod offices and convinced the officials that Camden needed a Swedish church for the immigrants, just as the Norwegians had Gethsemane Lutheran Church across the railroad tracks.

Grace was very active in church affairs. She sang in the choir, taught Sunday School, belonged to a circle, and was president of the Women's Missionary Society, among other things. Even when she was quite young, she organized the annual *smörgåsbord*. She also served as Salem's unofficial ambassador to newcomers. When special events or suppers were held, Lois Anderson said, Grace was always there. "She would work the line, finding out the names of people and their children, asking where they lived. She was the spirit of Salem."

One of Grace's favorite activities was helping at the Salem Church Dining Hall at the State Fair. The first dinners at the Fair were served in a tent in 1950. A permanent dining hall, used to this day, was built the next year. The dining hall does a thriving business during the twelve-day run of the fair and, until recent years, Grace was there. She died during the state fair in 2000. "We had to delay the funeral until after the fair," said Charlie, "because so many of the volunteers at the dining hall wanted to come."

At her funeral, on September 6, after the organ prelude of—very appropriately—"Amazing Grace," her grandson Andrew talked about her: "Ultimately, what really made Grace special is that she knew how to love other people, and that she knew how to make other people feel good about themselves and feel good about her as well."

I say "Amen" to that. Goodnight, Grace.

Grace's Egg Coffee

No Lutheran wedding or funeral in north Minneapolis was complete years ago without a lunch afterwards. "Egg coffee" was often served and was considered a cut above regular coffee because it was so clear. Grace advised keeping the coffee can (probably Folger's) in the refrigerator. If you don't have a coffee scoop, use a tablespoon of coffee for every two cups. The old fashioned pot has no inner mechanism; don't try to make this in a new-fangled pot! The recipe below is in her words.

"Place in old fashioned coffee pot one scant cup of water per cup wanted. Bring to boil. In small bowl place one coffee scoop (scoop is in coffee can) per two cups water used in pot, plus one additional scoop "for the pot." Before adding coffee to boiling water, stir into the coffee grounds enough beaten egg (along with shell or "skin" of shell if available) to thoroughly moisten the grounds. Stir moistened coffee into boiling water. Have it boil up, but not over. Then turn heat down and allow to brew several minutes. Pour about one-half cup cold water into spout to settle grounds and let sit briefly. (Store remaining beaten egg in covered dish/cup in refrigerator for next time.) Keep coffee warm on low burner.

Kroppkakor

(Swedish potato dumplings with pork fillings)

Makes eight or more dumplings

Grace Blomquist Anderson's recipe for this traditional Swedish specialty is in *Seasoned with Love,* a cookbook put out by Salem Church Women in 1994 in honor of the centennial in 1995.

5 c. russet potatoes, peeled and finely ground or
     processed (do not over-process)
1 c. (or more) flour
½ lb. salt pork, rinsed in cold water several times,
     diced and fried

Squeeze the potatoes dry. Work in about three-fourths cup of the flour by hand. Add more flour until it sticks together. Form half a baseball-sized portion of dough and put a walnut-sized cluster of the salt pork cubes in the center. Add more of the potato mix to form the other half of the "baseball" over the meat to completely enclose it. Place in simmering water in a large skillet for an hour.

Charlotte Lindquist Hansen
One of the Lindquist kids

Charlotte Lindquist Hansen is my friend Dave's mom, and that would be enough to make me like her. But I soon found out that, though she lives in St. Paul now and has for years, she is—like me—from the Camden neighborhood in north Minneapolis. That is our real bond. Charlotte is a generation older than I am, and the Camden I knew was very different from the Camden she grew up in. Still, it is fascinating—and comforting, somehow—to hear her talk about the old neighborhood.

Charlotte Hansen's parents, Selma Erickson Lindquist and Harry Lindquist, are at left and middle in the front row in this light-hearted photo. Charlotte's maternal grandparents are at left in the back. The woman at right in the back row is Emma Krefting, aunt of the author's friend, Ardis Krefting Anderson. Photo courtesy of Charlotte Hansen.

Charlotte was one of Harry and Selma Lindquist's kids. They lived across the railroad tracks from where I grew up and, because they were early Camden residents, they are connected with many other people I know or know of. So it's a little like talking to a long-lost cousin chatting with Charlotte. She knew the Blomquists [see Grace Blomquist Anderson's story] and her parents were very friendly with Emma Krefting, aunt of my friend Ardis Krefting Anderson.

Charlotte's dad's mother came from Småland with her parents when she was just two years old. "They came to Stillwater and walked to Taylor's Falls and homesteaded a mile from there," said Charlotte. "My grandmother came to the city and married my grandfather, who was a policeman. He witnessed a murder and was told to leave town." The Lindquists divorced—unusual in that day—and Charlotte's grandmother went back to the farm with her son, Harry. The Lindquists, Charlotte added, were very poor.

Later, her grandmother came back to Minneapolis and worked in a boarding house in Camden. There were many boarding houses in the late nineteenth and early twentieth centuries, as the neighborhood attracted lots of young, single immigrants who worked for the lumber mills on the Mississippi River. "My dad remembered seeing big logs come down the river," Charlotte said.

Charlotte's grandmother married again, and Charlotte thinks she may have met her husband when he lived at the boarding house. They moved back to the farm again after their marriage. When Harry was 14 or 15, he came back to Camden and worked in a butcher shop and grocery stores. "He learned the trade from Mr. Blomquist," said Charlotte. Mr. Blomquist was the father of Grace Blomquist, whose story appears in this chapter.

The C. A. Smith mill, in Camden, employed many immigrants and their families. Smith himself, despite his English-sounding name, was a Swedish immigrant. Photo courtesy of the Minneapolis Public Library, Minneapolis Collection.

Meanwhile, Selma Erickson and her parents—who were Norwegian—moved to Camden from northeast Minneapolis. "My mother grew up on 46th and Bryant. She used to carry lunches to her uncles who worked in the sawmill in Camden. That was on 44th Avenue. My mother went to Hamilton School," said Charlotte. Hamilton School is the common touchstone for old Camden kids. Charlotte went there, I went there, Ardis Krefting went there and Ardis' Aunt Emma, who also went there, told Ardis that she had to crawl across an icy plank over the creek in winter to get to school. The old building has long since been torn down, but Ardis has a yellow brick from it. It came from her family's brickyard further out on Lyndale Avenue North.

Charlotte Hansen's father, Harry Lindquist, had a butcher shop on 42nd and Fremont in Camden for many years. He is at right. Photo courtesy of Charlotte Hansen.

Selma Erickson's parents and others wanted a Norwegian Lutheran church and they got it: Gethsemane Lutheran was formed more than one hundred years ago. "The church was organized in my grandparents' house and it was built half a block down from their house. The young people later built a parish house where they could play basketball and have plays. They were ahead of their time," said Charlotte.

Harry the Swede met Selma the Norwegian one day. "He was working in a store on 46th and Lyndale and she came in to get warm, at least that's what she said," said Charlotte with a smile. Harry and Selma married—in Gethsemane—and went to live at 4622 Camden Avenue North.

Charlotte and her sisters, Alice and Ruth, played dress-up often when they were little girls. Their younger brothers, Rodger and Earle, also took part in the performances. "We had a great big mirror on the door in the hall. We paraded around and pretended we had weddings and we put on plays in front of it."

The Camden of Charlotte's early days was much more Scandinavian than in my time, although a Fourth of July parade emphasized that the sons and daughters of immigrants were American, too. "My mother would speak Norwegian to my dad and he would answer her in Swedish. He always had clerks who could speak Swedish when he had the shops. There would be people speaking Swedish and Norwegian on the streets," said Charlotte.

Sometimes Harry's relatives came down from the farm. "Once my great-grandmother—my father's grandmother—had to go to Bethesda Hospital. They brought her down on the wagon from the farm and she stayed with us later to recover. She wore high-button shoes and she couldn't speak any English."

Harry went on to have two of his own butcher and grocery shops with his partner, Frank Lindgren. Harry was famous for his 'Christmas sausage,' and also made a lot of potato sausage for the Christmas season. "He made potato sausage for Swedish Hospital at Christmas," said Charlotte. "He used to taste the raw sausage to see if it had enough seasoning and we'd say to him, 'Dad, you're going to die from eating that raw meat,' and he'd say he always spit it out." Harry wouldn't part with his recipe for the Christmas sausage. "He kept that to himself. He said we could never give it out to anyone until after he died."

Charlotte, Alice and Ruth grew up and married. Charlotte was a teacher before she married Henry Hansen in 1941 and had three boys—Trygg, Dave and Mark. Henry was a forestry professor at the University of Minnesota and the family spent most summers at the forestry and biological station in Itasca State Park.

As for Harry's recipe for Christmas sausage, the family finally gave it to a butcher in St. Anthony Park in St. Paul and every year it is available back in the meat counter at Speedy Market. Buy some—you'll like it!

Phyllis Johnson, taken for her Confirmation at Salem Lutheran Church in north Minneapolis. Her daughter Pixie Haug still has Phyllis' copy of "Luther's Little Catechism." Photo courtesy of the Elfstrom family.

Phyllis Johnson Elfstrom
Her heart was in Värmland

"There goes old man Johnson, out for his daily constitutional," my father said, as he glanced out of the window at Camden Park across the street. Curious (some would say downright nosey) even then, I ran to the window to look. Whether I watched him walking there more than once I don't remember, but in my mind's eye, I picture him on a cold afternoon, most likely in November, with the day turning fast to evening. There was no snow, only the bare trees and the dry leaves covering the ground. He wore a long, dark coat and a dark hat and strode briskly. In remembrance, he seems like a character in an Ingmar Bergman film. At the time, however, when I was five or six years old, I just knew he was our neighbor, a long-faced old man who looked both stern and sad to me.

Herman Johnson and his wife, Matilda "Tillie" Nelson Johnson, had lived in the little house with the screened front porch since they married in 1915. Herman was born and raised on a farm in Värmland and taught himself to sew as a young boy. He emigrated from Sweden with his three brothers—Carl, Oskar, and Adolf—early in the twentieth century. Adolf, whom the family always called *Bror* (brother) returned to Sweden but the others stayed. Herman worked as a tailor for years in the thriving Camden business community. He had a partner named Berg—the shop was called Johnson and Berg. "We never knew what Berg's first name was or where he lived," said Herman's granddaughter, Marci Elfstrom Osborne. "Berg did the fancy work. He was a buttonhole maker and he made buttonholes on suits for all the wealthy people in Minneapolis because he did such beautiful work."

Herman moved from house to house before he married Tillie, who was born in Minnesota of Swedish parents. Her mother—Christine Nelson, also a *Värmlänning*—ran one of the many boarding houses that catered to the young Swedish immigrants who flocked to the Camden community in north Minneapolis

Johnson and Berg's tailor shop in Camden, in north Minneapolis. Herman Johnson is second from right. Photo courtesy of the Elfstrom family.

around the beginning of the twentieth century. The Johnsons often played host to newcomers. "People would arrive at all hours from Sweden," said Marci Osborne. "They would come with Herman's name and address and say they were a friend of a friend of a friend in Sweden and Herman and Tillie would put them up until they found work. It usually didn't take them long. My Uncle Kenny used to tell me he would go to bed at night not knowing if he was going to wake up next to someone."

I don't remember knowing that the Johnsons were Swedish; they were just the neighbors. Herman died not long after I first remember seeing him on his walk. Perhaps it was the pain from his illness that made him look sad. Tillie stayed on in the house, visited occasionally by her children—Kenny and Phyllis and their families. Mrs. Johnson, a bulky woman who moved slowly because her ankles were swollen, was afraid we neighborhood kids would slide down the Dupont hill too fast or lose control of our trikes and wind up under the wheels of the cars and trucks that zoomed along Webber Parkway, a busy street. She was justified in worrying, but we thought she was crabby when she told us not to slide down the hill. My mother occasionally went to see her, but we children saw her less and less, and when she died, another link to a chapter in Camden history might have passed, if it hadn't been for Phyllis.

The Johnsons' daughter, Phyllis Elfstrom, and her family moved from their little bungalow in Crystal into the house after Tillie's death. Phyllis and Larry, who was nicknamed "Swede" though he was actually a mixture of nationalities, including Swedish, had three little girls—Kim, Marci, and Denise, who had been called Pixie ever since the nurses in the hospital where she was born said she looked just like a little pixie. A fourth daughter, Lauri, arrived many years later.

Phyllis was small and dainty, with curly light brown hair, a hearty laugh and the ability to make whoever she was talking to feel that he or she was her best friend. She was sympathetic and generous and had a knack for picking out just the right present for everyone. I still have a *dala* horse she gave me and a very glamorous pair of dangly lavender glass earrings. She has been dead for more than thirty years now, and I swear that all of Camden cried when she died, far too young and still without seeing her beloved Värmland.

Phyllis loved Sweden, and her ancestral province of Värmland in particular, with a steadfast devotion that did not diminish her equally strong sense of being an American one bit. She had a nice alto voice and often sang *Ack, Värmeland, du sköna, du härliga land*

From left, Marci Elfstrom Osborne, Kim Elfstrom Johnson, and Denise (Pixie) Elfstrom Haug. Photo courtesy of the Elfstrom family.

Traditonal Swedish Childrens' Night Prayer

Gud som haver barnen kär,
se till mig som liten är.
Vart jag mig i världen vänder,
står min lycka I Guds händer.
Lyckan kommer, lyckan går,
den Gud älskar, lyckan får.

(translation—Anne Gillespie Lewis)

God who holds children dear,
watch over me because I am small.
Wherever I turn in the world,
my happiness is in God's hands.
Happiness comes and happiness goes,
those God loves will have happiness

---

around the house and *Nu är det jul igen* when it was Christmastime. One year, when the Elfstroms had just brought their Christmas tree into the house, I happened to be there—as I often was, for I was the Elfstroms' babysitter as well as the neighbor girl—and she had all of us dance around the tree and sing *Nu är det jul igen och nu är det jul igen*. I was happy and intrigued, as our family's own Scandinavian traditions had dwindled to a Christmas Eve *smörgåsbord* and a few Norwegian phrases.

When Phyllis and Larry went out and I babysat, I listened to the older two—and Pixie when she could—say their nightly prayer in Swedish. They rattled off the words, and I don't think they really knew what they meant. Now—forty-five years later, I asked Marci if she remembered the prayer and with only the slightest hesitation, she repeated it. Of course, it didn't hurt that she had taken Swedish at the University of Minnesota in the intervening years.

Though she was the second generation born in the U.S. on her mother's side, Phyllis could speak *Värmländska*, the Värmland dialect of Swedish and could write it as well. She chatted away to her Uncle Carl and Auntie Esther *på Värmländska* and faithfully corresponded with cousins in Sweden, all the while thinking she would see it one day. She didn't travel much at all, though she got her pilot's license during World War II and sometimes talked knowledgeably and somewhat wistfully about her flying days and wind patterns and the like.

I, ever the listener, took it all in. Phyllis was busy with the girls and worked part-time from time to time, but always had time to "coffee" with the neighbors. I know she served as an escape valve for my mother, who was left a widow with six children—aged nine years to nine months—when my father died of a coronary thrombosis.

Phyllis Johnson in front of an airplane at Crystal Airport in the early 1940s. She worked in the office there and took lessons. She got her pilot's license without telling her parents she was doing it and she arranged to have her brother drive them out to the airport one day. When they arrived, he pointed to a plane over the airport and they said, "See that plane? Phyllis is flying it." Photo courtesy of the Elfstrom family.

I remember Phyllis as a rather indifferent cook, but she always made Swede sausage (potato sausage, as the Swedes themselves call it) at Christmastime. She bought real beef intestines for the sausage casings and the sausage production took at least a day. She didn't have a real sausage stuffer and instead turned an angel food pan upside-down and pushed the casing end on the end of the narrow tube in the center, holding it firmly with one hand and raising the pan and casing up above her shoulder, much as the Statue of Liberty holds the torch. Miss Liberty, however, isn't stuffing sausage meat by the handful into the torch! When each casing was full, she pulled it off the angel food pan, folded the ends in, and started on another one.

She was stuffing sausage, facing a window, when my mother first came to call on her. "Excuse me," said my mother, "but what in the world are you doing?" Their friendship started that day and continued for the next 15 years until Phyllis' death from a brain hemorrhage when she was 47 years old. I said that all of Camden cried when she died, but I have changed my mind— I am sure the skies in Värmland wept as copiously as the people of Camden when they heard the news.

Time has passed and Camden is no longer recognizably Swedish, although Salem Evangelical Lutheran Church still anchors the corner of Dupont and 42nd Avenues North. The Elfstrom girls are scattered and even I have moved across the Mississippi River. Marci Osborne is keeper of the legacy, though all the girls are aware of their heritage and have wonderful memories of their mother and their neighborhood. Marci has been to Värmland and so have I. And Phyllis would be pleased—but hardly surprised—to know that my own children, who are a bare one-sixteenth Swedish, have also sung *Nu är det jul igen* around the Christmas tree.

Nu är det jul igen

Nu är det jul igen,
och nu är det jul igen
och julen vara ska till påska.
Det var inte sant
och det var inte sant
för däremellan kommer fasta.

---

translation:

Now it's Christmas again,
now it's Christmas again,
and Christmas lasts until Easter.
No, that's not true,
no, that's not true,
because Lent comes in between.

Phyllis Johnson Elfstrom and her youngest daughter,
Lauri. This picture was taken several months before
Phyllis died. Photo courtesy of the Elfstrom family.

In this old photo, women in the Rättvik style of dress are shown dancing. Rättvik is in the province of Dalarna, in central Sweden. Lake Siljan is in the background. Photo courtesy of the American Swedish Institute.

Chapter Two

So Far Away in the World

In 1954, Nils Gustavsson in Sweden wrote to his relatives in St. Paul saying *"Du förstår det skulle vara roligt få veta litet om sina släktingar så långt borta i världen"* (You understand that it would be nice to know a little about relatives so far away in the world).[1] Although commercial air travel was expanding in the middle of the twentieth century, it was still uncommon for immigrants and their sons and daughters to make the trip back to Sweden. Letters were still the most common means of contact. Here are letters that reveal something of the immigrant mindset, although—as can be seen between the lines of John Wallberg's letters—sometimes they did not tell the whole truth.

Bertha Brunius
A light heart on the frontier

Letters were important to Swedish immigrants. One early Swedish immigrant who was dying for news of Sweden was Bertha Brunius. Her playful letter is dated 26 March, 1856, under a return address of "St. Anthony Falls, Minnesota," which was then separate but is now part of the city of Minneapolis. She also makes the notation "My address from now on / St. Anthony / Minnesota Territory / U.S. of America" above the salutation. The letter, portions of which appear below, was translated into English by an unknown person. The translation is in the American Swedish Institute's archives.[2] Bertha apparently was not at St. Anthony for long. The land that she mentions her husband buying was probably in Carver County, for there are many records of Oswald and Bertha Brunius and their family living in Carver. Despite her references to Sweden, Bertha's obituary says she was born in Germany.[3] After her death, her daughter, Mrs. C. A. Widstrand, donated $1,000 to the Presbyterian church in Carver "in memory of my beloved mother."[4] The letter, which has been edited for length, contradicts the usual image of the immigrants enduring hardships and being depressed. Prof. Teddy Brunius, of Uppsala, Sweden, who is an art historian and is related to Bertha's husband, notes that Bertha's letter presents a much happier picture of the new immigrant than most readers might imagine. "It is a charming letter," Prof. Brunius wrote. "It is remarkable how optimistic it is, much more than you would find among the immigrants in Vilhelm Moberg's novels."[5]

"My dearly beloved, but naughty friends!

   Do you wicked little children think that you have the right to ignore me in the way you have done this past year? Do you think I shall ever forgive you for forgetting me in such a heartless manner? . . . how endlessly I long for news from Stockholm and you.

. . . I traveled with my little Laura in the middle of October from Dubuque to this place. Oswald met us in St. Paul, but we went nine English miles further up to where we now live, as Oswald thinks it will be better for us in the future. St. Anthony is only five years old, has 4,000 inhabitants, and lies along the Mississippi. On the other side of the river lies the city of Minneapolis, one year old, with 1,000 inhabitants. Both cities are united by a remarkably beautiful suspension bridge of steel cables, 620 feet long, the first over the Mississippi. The first winter was very cold, 50 degrees below zero, shortly before Christmas, but nevertheless I like Minnesota's climate very much. We have never been so healthy. Here we have such a clean, clear, fresh air, and always sunshine; now we have splendid spring weather, and all the snow is gone.

The climate is like that of Sweden. That may be the reason that there are so many from the dear land of Sweden living here. All our friends are Swedes. A young Swedish girl, Emma Widstrand (a minister's daughter from Närke) who arrived here shortly after I did, has lived with me the whole winter and is still with me. You can't understand how happy I have been to have her with me, as she came directly from Stockholm with her brother, who worked in the trust department of a bank there. Perhaps my mother's brother Carl knows him; he must at least have seen him.

. . . My kind good friends, shall I ever see you again? Have you definitely decided whether or not you will come to this country? Perhaps you are already on your way, and the reason you have not written to me is that you plan to surprise me . . . Has Emelie at Arvidsons' come back? . . . let me hear soon why you, my little Gike, who used to write so much, have stopped writing to me. Are you angry at me? In my letter to you I also enclosed a letter to Gustava and Laura. Have they received it? Why doesn't Laura write? Mr. Widstrand told me at Christmas time that his friend Hallgren had written that Harold Moller had died, but now he believed this news was incorrect, and that it was Pulkon who had died. Which is it? I don't believe that there will be any deep sorrow at the death of either one of them.

A Mr. Polman wrote that on March 10 he would leave New York for a few weeks' visit to Sweden. He offered to take letters to me with him on the return trip. My dear ones, please send him with many long letters to me, and several Swedish newspapers . . .

Perhaps Tilda will come to this country at the same time as Polman returns. She wanted to accompany the Widstrands last fall, but her brother (in the post office) didn't want her to go to America. Sweet gals, give Tilda heartfelt greetings from me and Emma Widstrand. How are Uncle Carl and his children? Have any one of them married? And Pihlgrens, Rylanders, Didricks, Mollers, Lidse, old lady Regnstrand, and all my other friends. No one named, no one forgotten!

Don't show this letter to anyone, *as it is carelessly put together, as I am so absent minded, and Laura walks around me from one side to the other, wanting me to take her on my knee. The little one is so good, and now that she can walk and is beginning to talk, and understands everything we say, she is our great delight.*

. . . Last fall Oswald brought 70 acres of most beautiful land 17 miles from here [this was apparently in Carver], *along the shores of a large inland lake for $3 an acre. Now it is already worth from $10 to $15. Building lots in the city have gone up similarly. The waterfalls which are here have done much to spend the rise in value.*

Now, my beloved friends, I close this time with a prayer that you will not let me wait long for a reply . . . Many, many greetings . . . and a thousand kisses from your devoted Bertha Brunius."

This is the first bridge over the Mississippi River, not just in Minnesota, anywhere on the river. Bertha Brunius wrote about it in a letter to Sweden in 1856. The bridge was opened in 1855. Photo courtesy of the Minneapolis Public Library, Minneapolis Collection.

In the margin, she wrote

"*. . . Are you acquainted with burgomaster Eklund's wife in Stockholm who is a niece of Colonel Hall (a daughter of his sister)? She has written to them that some of my friends in Stockholm told her that I was not only charming but also very pretty. Who is responsible for this dreadful slander? I have been pondering in vain, racking my brains, as I didn't know I had any enemies in Stockholm.*"

Professor Teddy Brunius, who was a visiting professor at Grinnell College in Iowa in the mid-fifties and is related to Bertha's husband, had another letter concerning the family translated by Prof. Grace Hunter during his stay in Iowa. The letter, and his introduction, appeared in the *Bulletin* of the American Swedish Institute. The letter was written by Johan Niklas Brunius to his brother, Carl Georg Brunius in Sweden. In it, Johan Brunius describes the journey to Carver from New York and also the settlement where Oswald and Bertha Brunius lived after their stay in St. Anthony:

"*. . . We began our journey with 30 miles on the Hudson River, then by train to the Mississippi River, on which we traveled 300 miles by steamship. We finished the journey with about 20 miles on the Minnesota River.*
Carver, the town where the children live, is a little new town still in its childhood; its surroundings, consisting of beautiful hardwood forests and extensive meadows, are beautiful. The river contributes not a little to the city's beautiful appearance. There is vivacity, too, through the frequent traffic of ships. The population consists, for the greater part, of Americans and Germans and some few Swedes. The postmaster is Swedish. There is even a Swedish shopkeeper, by the name of Cronsioe, who is from Scania."[6]

Albin E. Johnson
An immigrant's paper trail

Carole Neumann's Uncle Al Johnson, her uncle by marriage, was a nice guy who is remembered fondly by Carole and her family. In most respects, Uncle Al was

Al Johnson served in France for the United States during the First World War, but he didn't get back to Sweden until 63 years after he left in 1913. Photo courtesy of the American Swedish Institute.

no different from most Swedish immigrants. He emigrated from Småland, as did many others. He came to Minneapolis and stayed with relatives at first, like so many newcomers. He served in World War I and later worked as a milkman for Northland Creamery—one of many Swedish immigrants to do so. He met his wife, Alma, at a dance, where so many romances bloomed among young Scandinavian couples in the early part of the twentieth century. And, like so many immigrants who wanted one more look at his homeland, he made one visit back to Sweden, just three years before he died in 1979.

What makes Al Johnson's story a little different from that of most immigrants is that he was a saver. He salted away many documents that give a clear picture of his life—from his early days in Småland to his new home in Minnesota. His paper treasures document his school days, immigration and service in World War I. The documents and artifacts were donated to the archives of the American Swedish Institute by Carole after the deaths of her uncle and aunt and their daughter, who was the Johnson's only child and died childless.[7] To follow Uncle Al's trail from Småland to Minneapolis is to follow in the footsteps of all Swedish immigrants of the same era. Like many immigrants, his last name is spelled differently in different documents and earlier he was known by a completely different last name. This, too, is a story that is often told.

At right is the landing card for Albin Johansson [Johnson]. The instructions read: "When landing at New York this card to be pinned to the coat or dress of the passenger in a prominent position." Document courtesy of the American Swedish Institute.

S.S. "ADRIATIC."
From LIVERPOOL 8th November, 1913.
MANIFEST SHEET NO.
22
NAME.
Johansson Albin
LIST No. 7   See Back.

NOTICE.

ENGLISH.
When landing at New York this card to be pinned to the coat or dress of the passenger in a prominent position.

SWEDISH.
Vid ankomsten till New York måste detta kort fastsättas på rocken eller klädningen så att det kan latt observeras.

FRENCH.
En débarquant à New York cette carte doit être fixée sur le paletôt ou la robe du passager de sorte qu'elle soit bien en vue.

GERMAN.
Bei der Ankunft in New York muss diese Karte auf der Auszenseite des Rockes oder der Kleidung befestigt werden, wo es deutlich zu sehen ist.

ITALIAN.
Disbarcando a New York questa carta deve essere appuntata al vestito del passagero in una posizione visibile.

FINNISH.
Kuin tulette New York niin pankaa tama lippu rintaane.

CROATIAN.
Kada dajdem u New York ta karta maram uzet na svojem kapotu za imit gatovo.

DUTCH.
Op arriveeren en New York deze kaart most zyn zo wiyzen aangemacht op het rock om te zien klaar.

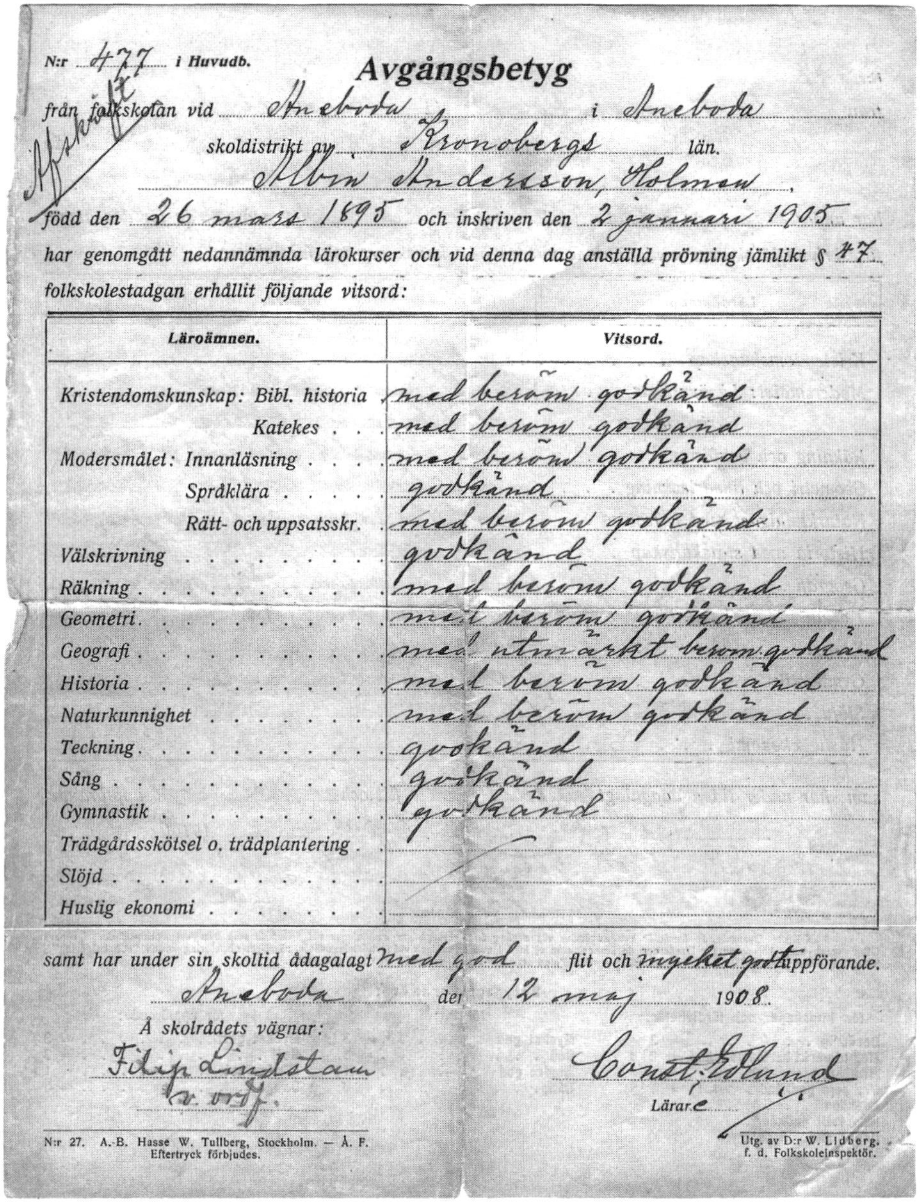

Avgångsbetyg

N:r 477 i Huvudb.

från folkskolan vid Aneboda i Aneboda

skoldistrikt av Kronobergs län.

Albin Andersson, Holman,

född den 26 mars 1895 och inskriven den 2 januari 1905

har genomgått nedannämnda lärokurser och vid denna dag anställd prövning jämlikt § 47

folkskolestadgan erhållit följande vitsord:

Läroämnen.	Vitsord.
Kristendomskunskap: Bibl. historia	med beröm godkänd
Katekes	med beröm godkänd
Modersmålet: Innanläsning	med beröm godkänd
Språklära	godkänd
Rätt- och uppsatsskr.	med beröm godkänd
Välskrivning	godkänd
Räkning	med beröm godkänd
Geometri	med beröm godkänd
Geografi	med utmärkt beröm godkänd
Historia	med beröm godkänd
Naturkunnighet	med beröm godkänd
Teckning	godkänd
Sång	godkänd
Gymnastik	godkänd
Trädgårdsskötsel o. trädplantering	
Slöjd	
Huslig ekonomi	

samt har under sin skoltid ådagalagt med god flit och mycket god uppförande.

Aneboda den 12 maj 1908.

Å skolrådets vägnar:

Filip Lindstam v. ordf.

Const. Edlund Lärare

N:r 27. A.-B. Hasse W. Tullberg, Stockholm. — Å. F. Eftertryck förbjudes.

Utg. av D:r W. Lidberg, f. d. Folkskoleinspektör.

This school-leaving certificate from Sweden showed that Al Johnson was a good student. Document courtesy of the American Swedish Institute.

Nearly five years after he arrived in the United States, Albin E. Johnson became a U.S. citizen. Document courtesy of the American Swedish Institute.

Al Johnson is not just a historically significant stack of papers and artifacts. "He always came across as very warm," said Carole about her uncle. "You always knew he liked you. He was really good with kids. He was quiet-natured. I never heard him raise his voice. He was just so happy to be in America."

Yes, he was happy to be in America, but if circumstances had been different he would have remained in Sweden. That's what he told Robert Owen of *Smålandsposten*, who interviewed him on his return to Sweden in 1976, after 63 years away. The excerpt from the interview below, published on July 19, 1976, was in Swedish except where Al mixed in some English. It was translated by Anne Gillespie Lewis:

"Today I wouldn't have emigrated. Not if I were 17 years old in today's Sweden. No, sir. I would have stayed here in this country [Sweden] to seek the adventure that I once sought in the States 63 years ago. But on the other hand, if the clock could be turned back to 1913, I wouldn't have had any doubt again. I would have emigrated. For then it was America that offered the adventure. I have not regretted my life for one minute. It's America I love, not Sweden."[8]

Uncle Al—then known as Albin Andersson—was a bright kid, but not outstanding, according to the marks on his school leaving certificate. His best marks were in geography and arithmetic and bookkeeping, while he was not so hot in art, choir and gymnastics. He got top marks *(Mycket gott)* for his conduct, and earned a "good" mark in industriousness. He left school in 1908, when he was 13 years old, was confirmed the next year, and in 1913 took off for America.

The official document giving permission for "Albin Emanuel Johanesson" to emigrate is dated October 31, 1913. The all-important immigration contract, his passage to the new world, is dated November 8, 1913. For 264 Swedish Kronor, White Star Lines agreed to transport "Albin Emanuel Johanisson" (note the different spelling) from Malmö, on Sweden's south coast, to Minneapolis, Minnesota, by way of Liverpool and New York. He saved both the landing card and the inspection card issued by the ship, the *S.S. Adriatic*. The ship left Liverpool November 13th and arrived at Ellis Island in New York, on November 23rd—a ten-day journey.

By the time Uncle Al applied for citizenship, he was known as Albin Johnson and he remained Albin Johnson the rest of his days. On his declaration of intention to file for citizenship, Uncle Al sounds like quite a dish. He was nearly six feet tall, slim, blond and blue-eyed. He became a citizen on Aug. 1, 1916, shortly after he was drafted into the Army. He served in France and escaped unscathed and undecorated. He kept a 1919 form letter from John J. Pershing, Commander in Chief of the American Expeditionary Forces thanking him, as a fellow soldier, for his service. The letter said, in part:

"In leaving the scenes of your victories, may I ask that you carry home your high ideals and continue to live as you have served—an honor to the principles for which you have fought and to the fallen comrades you leave behind.

It is with pride in our success that I extend to you my sincere thanks for your splendid service to the army and to the nation."

Years later, the former Private Johnson received a certificate of thanks for his military service from President Jimmy Carter. And here the paper trail ends—no more life-changing documents. However, it seems that Uncle Al did continue to live as he had served, a quiet, unassuming milkman who had satisfied his youthful yen for adventure.

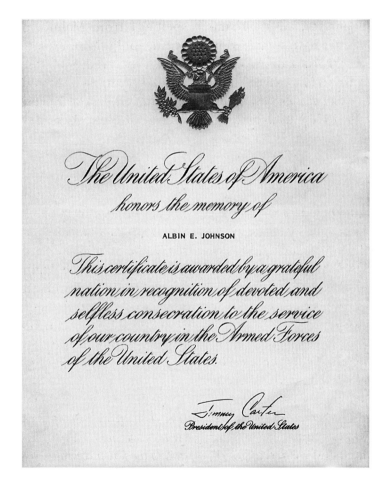

Al Johnson received this certificate of thanks from President Jimmy Carter for his service in World War I. Document courtesy of American Swedish Institute.

The Twin Cities Folk Dancers paused for a formal portrait sometime in the 1920s. Front, left to right, are Linnea Osman, Hedvig Johnson and Alice Linder. Back, from left, are Ragnar Johnson, Oscar Johnson, John Wallberg, Gunnar Walter, Gunhild Anderson and Knute Linder. Photo courtesy of Lorraine McGrath.

John P. Wallberg
"Next Christmas I'll be home"

John Wallberg, whose story is recounted through his daughter Lorraine's eyes in the chapter on Swedes at Play, wrote letters home to Sweden from the year he left, 1912, until he died 24 years later. Lorraine Wallberg McGrath wasn't aware of the existence of the letters until her cousin in Sweden, Åke Wallberg, sent her copies of some of them in 1994. The letter of Christmas, 1912, written from Fort Frances, Canada, is printed below in its entirety. The other letters were written from St. Paul, Minnesota.[9] Translation by Anne Gillespie Lewis.

Fort Frances, Dec. 25, 1912

Dear parents and brothers and sisters!

It is now Christmas night as I sit here and write these lines. I have worked the whole day but it didn't go so well because my thoughts were too much in Sweden and at home with you. Yes, that was the first Christmas I was away from you and the first Christmas that I worked and the last, I hope. Did you miss me? Lucky that I had work, otherwise it probably would have been harder, because I would have had time to think about you more!

I, along with a boy from Norrköping, am at a small, new railway station. It isn't open for passengers yet, up to now only freight trains drive there. We don't get letters more than once a week, so it is still best to send letters to Winnipeg, because the conductor usually goes in and picks up letters.

I never thought that it would be so hard to be away on Christmas. I try to think about it as little as possible but that is

impossible. My friend Eric is in the same situation. He's got a mother in Sweden and a fiancée. Last evening when we were eating, we didn't know what we should do, then I said to Eric that we should go lie down so that we would sleep away our gloomy thoughts, but sleep wouldn't come and free us so we had to fill our pipes and smoke until our heads were whirling when I fell asleep. This morning we were up at four o'clock because we begin our work then and keep on until six P.M. There is not much to do, so one doesn't get tired.

If you had as beautiful Christmas weather as we have that would be nice. Here in the woods there is a lot of snow, little cold and complete quiet.

I haven't got any mail here since I left Winnipeg. Maybe I have some in Winnipeg, but it hasn't come here yet. This is only about 250 miles from Winnipeg, but the railroad is still new and hasn't provided for the mail yet.

As I sit here and think, I don't regret that I left but I won't be away another Christmas. No! Next Christmas I'll be home with all of you. There will be so much great joy.

I must close now because I can't write more because I am not in the mood to write because I am too sad.

A thousand kind regards to you all and all relatives from your son and brother,

John

He mentioned going home again in several letters, but never got there. In an early, undated letter, he writes:

". . . Maybe there will be a trip over for me in the future, if everything goes as I think."

In March of 1921, he writes,

"I had almost had it in mind to travel to Sweden this summer, but it costs so terribly [much]. One can't come home empty handed either and just the journey there and back costs over 400 dollars, so one has to have so much extra for such a trip . . . if I go no one will know about it until I am on my way."

The following year, he writes:

"Certainly I think about seeing how you have it. If we're all spared, it could be pretty soon. I've heard it said that the shipping company is coming down in its prices next summer and if so, better have the pancakes and meatballs ready because they'll disappear when I come."

In July of 1936, less than six months before he died, and knowing he was ill, he still held onto the dream of returning home:

"I had wanted to visit you this summer, but conditions are such that one doesn't know what is going to happen! Presidential election in fall and uncertain times and the longer one puts off the journey the longer it takes to make up one's mind. It will be some time! If YOU have the time and opportunity to visit us, you are heartily welcome . . ."

There was much more in the letters—mentioning his dance group, talking about his two children, boasting slightly about the United States, chiding his parents for not saving money, inquiring about acquaintances.

During the drought of 1936, he wrote:

". . . In Dakota the grasshoppers ate up everything there was to eat and then they piled themselves up into fifteen- to twenty-foot high stacks. Then hail came in its turn and destroyed and killed them. Now you'll say again 'liar' and 'how American'—but it's true. To write about something that happens here is so thankless because it sounds so unbelievable for people who have never seen or are unfamiliar with American conditions."

John Wallberg gave a piggy back ride to two-year-old Lorraine on a summer day at Forest Lake. Photo courtesy of Lorraine McGrath.

He wrote about his children:

"Harold will be two years old on Thursday. I wish you could see him!!"

When his daughter was born, he wrote:

"My sweet little girl is named Thelma Lorraine and is called Thelma."

John Wallberg also philosophized about America and Sweden. In an undated letter, probably written in 1916, he writes:

"I spoke about offers. Yes, you better believe that's triple. It's not like in Sweden that one who is the poorest has to keep in his corner. No! Here we're all equal."

Later, apparently more ambivalent about America's opportunities, he writes:

". . . little Sweden is now presented as an example for America's future in regard to its cooperative movements and organizations. Yes, there is scarcely a day that there isn't an article in the daily paper and showing the correct system in the business and other pages. I have never been and never will be bashful or ashamed of being Swedish but there comes a time when one is really proud to be called a 'Swede.'"

His letters show a sense of time passing and his gradual "Americanization:"

". . . I have thought many times about how life would have shaped for me if I had stayed . . ."

". . . I got your latest letter yesterday and it woke me up a bit—I saw that Agnes Höglund ended her days. I can still remember the morning I left Gävle and I can still see all three of you before my eyes. That was the last I saw of Agnes and she was then just a little girl. That's the way it goes—some go young and some old . . ."

". . . I have forgotten a great deal from Sweden in the 24 years I have been away . . ."

and, poignantly, in a postscript to one letter

"P.S. I have now read through what I wrote and notice that the style is not as it should be—am I forgetting how to write Swedish? That should scarcely surprise me now when I have so much to do with my new adopted tongue."

His letters are full of references to friends and relatives and, always, he ends with many greetings:

"Now greet all acquaintances and relatives and friends and greet especially my dear parents and brother and best greetings to Arne and John and to you hearty greetings." He closes it, in English, *"From your brother, John,"* and adds, also in English, *"Write soon again. Don't forget."*

Ewa Söderström Rydåker, with her mother Svea, and her brother Håkan. Photo courtesy of Ewa Rydåker.

Chapter Three

The New Newcomers

The few Swedes who lived in Minnesota in Bertha Brunius' time swelled to thousands in the late nineteenth and earliest twentieth centuries. Sweden, so poor compared to the wealthy country we know today, lost approximately one-fourth of its residents to emigration. Only Norway, Iceland and Ireland had higher emigration rates.[1] In the early days, a ticket to America was a one-way passage. Very few immigrants had the money to go back for a visit. Bonds between family members stretched and stretched and sometimes broke. Some families wrote letters often, but as the immigrants here began to lose their Swedish language skills, that, too, declined. Many families lost touch completely with their relatives, but recent interest in genealogy and the ease of travel have brought many long-lost cousins together again.

Over the years, emigration from Sweden has slowed to a trickle. Most of the recent Swedish immigrants in the Twin Cities today came because of work or came to study or work temporarily and wound up staying. Some—mainly women—married Americans. Below are the stories of several modern immigrants.

Ewa and Anders Rydåker
Living in two worlds

Unlike the Swedes of an earlier era, Ewa and Anders Rydåker represent a new kind of immigrant, who comes to the United States on business or to study and may or may not decide to stay. The Rydåkers lived in Minnesota while their two daughters were growing up, returned to Sweden for more than three years, and are now back, living in Roseville, a suburb of St. Paul. Family, friends, business and education beckon them back to Sweden often, but they spend most of their time in Minnesota. Will they return to Sweden permanently? Possibly. Will they stay in Minnesota? Maybe. They are truly people who live in two different worlds at the same time.

In the old days, Swedes emigrated from "the old country" to the new land of America and returned only if they were lucky enough to afford a vacation. Many died in their adopted land without ever returning to see parents, other relatives and friends. The new immigrants have had a far different experience. Ewa Rydåker probably can't count the number of times she and Anders have flown over the Atlantic. In recent years, the thrill of a newborn granddaughter, plus sad occasions—the illnesses and deaths of his father and her mother and other family matters—have increased the number of trips back and forth. "I have really never been away from Sweden for more than a year," Ewa said. The travelling to and from Sweden a year or so ago grew grim as her mother's condition worsened, and her death, though not unexpected, was sudden enough that Ewa was not able to make it back to Sweden before she died. "As you might imagine, it was so difficult when my mother passed away," she said.

In the late nineteenth and early twentieth centuries, many Swedes had "America Fever," partly inspired by the glowing reports of relatives who had emigrated. By the latter half of the twentieth century, however, Sweden had prospered and America was no longer the golden lure it once was. Ewa never thought much about it when she was growing up in Uppsala, an hour north of Stockholm. "Oh, you read about America in the schools, but what I mainly can recall knowing about it is movie stars and popular TV series. There was only one person on dad's side who went to America. We never talked about it that much until I met Anders because he had relatives over here. Before we got married, we went to visit his relatives in Detroit. My first impression of the United States was that everything was bigger and that people were so friendly."

Ewa and Anders married in their mid-twenties and settled in Uppsala. Their two girls—Sofie and Louise—were born there. Ewa worked for SAS (Scandinavian Airlines System) and Anders, an engineer by training, went to work for an innovative energy consulting company that opened an office in St. Paul, Minnesota. When the girls were eight and eleven, Anders was offered a one-year temporary job in the St. Paul office of District Energy. The decision was hard to make. "The girls and I cried and cried and thought that it was such a big step," said Ewa. After they had decided to leave Sweden, the girls went once a week to practice English with an American lady. "Sofie learned a few words, like cat, and dog, and horse. The girls liked it because they got Oreo cookies and milk."

Ewa and Anders Rydåker posed with their daughters, Louise, left, and Sofie, right, as they left their house in Sweden to come to America. Photo courtesy of Ewa Rydåker.

They left Sweden in 1983. "We kept saying, 'Well, it's just a year,'" said Ewa. They rented a house in Roseville at first. One year turned into another and then another and then another, until the Rydåkers had been in Roseville seven years. The girls attended Brimhall Elementary in Roseville, which was a little United Nations. "The kids in that school spoke 32 different languages. Mom and dad came over once and went to a party at school where they celebrated all the different cultures."

Ewa found it a bit harder to adjust. She had studied English in school and spoken it during the time she lived briefly in England. Still, she said, "I had a headache every day from listening to the news." She couldn't work, because she didn't have a work permit. She was busy with the girls and their school, but she also took classes at the University of Minnesota. "I knew I had to take care of myself, so I went straight to the 'U.'" One of the classes, in English as a Second Language, helped her with English. She also took French classes, building on the French she knew from Sweden. Later she helped out at the school with the ESL program. She is still conscious of her accent, "I feel that I still have an accent and I am very anxious to speak properly." Ewa is also conscious of not being from the United States. "I know I'm not from here, so I try to follow what others do." The one thing she does not do is cook like most Americans. "I still stick with the Swedish way," said Ewa.

Ewa, a cheerful, friendly person, made friends with other expatriate Swedes and immigrants. Gunhild and Hilding Anderson, she said, "were like mom and dad to me." She is active in SWEA-Minnesota, the local chapter of a worldwide association of Swedish-speaking women, and also the American Swedish Institute. Concerned that her kids were forgetting their Swedish, she and nine other women started *Svenska Skolan,* which met on Saturday mornings to let children use or learn Swedish in a relaxed, playful setting.

Ewa remains surprised at the number of Minnesotans who identified themselves to her as Swedish. "I've heard so many people say, 'Oh, my grandma is from Sweden' or 'I'm a quarter Swedish and a quarter this and a quarter that.'" At first, she felt Swedish-Americans didn't seem remotely like the Swedes she knew back home, but sometimes, she said, after being around them for a time,

Ewa Söderström Rydåker, right, was the Lucia at this program in 1962 in Sweden. Photo courtesy of Ewa Rydåker.

they did seem to bear more resemblance in their ways to their Swedish cousins many times removed. "I was surprised to see how some of the old traditions were kept up. Everything they tell me about the old days here is fascinating to hear. There are many similar stories. They are all interesting, but sometimes sad."

Ewa and her country are often linked in the same sentence. "I do feel some people I meet think it's interesting that I'm from Sweden." Sometimes, however, the charm of being a novelty fades. "They always say, 'This is Ewa from Sweden.' Why don't they just say 'This is Ewa?'"

She does wish that Americans in general knew more about Sweden. Even Swedish-Americans often have the wrong idea of current Sweden, she has found. "They don't realize in all the years since their ancestors left Sweden that things have changed," she said. The poor country that couldn't support its mainly rural population has transformed into a very urban, well-off, technically sophisticated society.

In 1990, Ewa and Anders and the girls returned to Sweden. They expected that they wouldn't be back, except on visits. The American experiment had been interesting, but it seemed to be over. Sofie had graduated from Roseville High School and was about to start college in Sweden and Louise was about to enter high school when they moved back. Four years later, the president of the company Anders had worked for as a consultant in St. Paul died suddenly and Anders was offered his position. Again, the decision was difficult. And again, they decided to leave Sweden, with the entire family returning to another house in Roseville in 1994. Louise went to the University of Minnesota and Sofie finished her Uppsala University degree through long-distance studies while working. Seven years after moving back to Minnesota again, their lives are full. Both girls now live in Sweden. Ewa and Anders have become grandparents and they are still very active in business, civic and Swedish-American affairs. For the time being, their lives are lived primarily in Minnesota but the lines of communication are literally always open. "The kids consider themselves Swedish, but I live in America. Even though the girls are there, the telephone rates are going down," Ewa said with a laugh.

Although she is now very comfortable with American ways, she does not feel like an American herself. "My heart is still in Sweden. We have kept up with all our old friends. When I go there, I fit in right away."

Rhubarb Cream

This rhubarb sauce is a familiar Swedish summer treat. Serve warm or cold topped with milk. This recipe is based on one in *Vår kokbok* (Rabén & Sjögren). Used by permission.

Serves four
4 to 6 good-sized rhubarb stalks, peeled if they are old
1½ c. water
⅓ c. sugar, plus extra sugar for sprinkling on top
2½ tbsp. (less for a more liquid sauce) cornstarch or
    potato starch

In a medium saucepan, bring water and sugar to a boil. Add rhubarb, cover, turn heat down a bit and cook until rhubarb is tender. While the rhubarb is cooking, put cornstarch or potato starch in a small bowl and add one to two tablespoons of water. Mix thoroughly. Add cornstarch mixture to the rhubarb gradually, stirring as you add it. Let the rhubarb come to a boil again and boil just a minute or so. Remove from heat. Sprinkle sugar to taste on top before serving.

A Taste of Home

Ewa Rydåker was brought up in Uppsala, Sweden, and moved here for the first time when she was grown and had two children. She and her husband went back to Sweden for a few years and now are back in Roseville again. She is often hungry for particular foods from Sweden and most of them—including one of her favorites, *Matjes* herring—can now be found in some large supermarkets here. For specialty items, including *Västerbotten* cheese and Swedish syrups, she goes to Ingebretsen Scandinavian Foods in Minneapolis. The recipe below, for meringue torte, needs no special ingredients. It is a Swedish favorite and there are many variations of it. The trick to the recipe is greasing the parchment paper very well and patiently spreading the cake batter evenly over it. If you like, add a couple drops of vanilla and a teaspoon of sugar to the whipped cream.

Pinocciotårta

(meringue torte)

This recipe is from *Sju sorters kakor*, published by ICA förlaget AB. translated by Ewa Rydåker and Anne Gillespie Lewis and used by permission.

Serves 12
for the cake:
  ⅓ c. butter, at room temperature
  ¾ c. plus 2 tbsp. powdered sugar
  5 egg yolks
  ½ c. plus 2 tbsp. flour
  1½ tsp. baking powder
  4 tbsp. milk
for the meringue:
  5 egg whites
  ¾ c. plus 2 tbsp. sugar
  ⅓ c. sliced almonds
for the filling:
  1½ c. whipping cream
  1 c. fresh or frozen raspberries (optional)
  strawberries for decoration (optional)

Preheat the oven to 325 degrees. In a medium bowl, cream the butter and powdered sugar together. Add egg yolks, one at a time, stirring well after each addition. Mix the flour and baking powder together and add, alternating with the milk, to the butter and egg mix. Stir well. Cover the bottom of a 10- by 15-in. pan with parchment paper and grease well or spray with non-stick spray. Spread the cake batter evenly over the paper. It will be very thin. Dip a knife or spatula periodically in hot water, then wipe off the excess water, to make it easier to spread the batter. Set aside. In a medium bowl, beat the egg whites to stiff peaks. Fold in the sugar. Beat for another minute or two. Spread the meringue gently over the cake batter. It doesn't need to be even. Sprinkle the almonds on top and bake for approximately 20 minutes, or until the meringue feels dry. Cool and peel parchment paper off. Cut cake in half. Drain berries if using frozen berries. Whip the cream and fold in berries. Put filling between cake halves and decorate with strawberries around the cake, if desired.

When she visits friends and relatives in Sweden, Mariann Tiblin often travels by bus. Photo courtesy of Mariann Tiblin.

Mariann Tiblin
Minneapolis resident, citizen of the world

Mariann Tiblin has set the table for the two of us in the sunny and cozy dining room she calls her Dalarna room. Against one wall is a magnificent wooden cabinet, painted in the traditional bold *dalmålning* style with flowers and the date "1812." It used to be in her par-ents' home in Borlänge, Sweden, in the province of Dalarna. On the walls of the room are several paintings, one of a stylized *dala* horse that has become the unofficial symbol of Sweden. Outside the second floor of the south Minneapolis duplex where we sit, trees wave their new leaves and the scent of lilacs perfumes the air.

A cinnamon-sprinkled rice pudding, accompanied by a dish with cranberry sauce to spoon atop the pudding, and a loaf of newly baked bread are on the table. And, of course, there is a full coffee pot in the kitchen, from which she refills our cups throughout the afternoon. Rice pudding is usually made for Christmas in Sweden, but Mariann has made this for me because I asked if she had a recipe.

It is early May, nearly six weeks after the date Mariann considers her special day.

"April first, April Fools' Day, is the anniversary of my arrival here thirty-three years ago. That's the day I walked into Walter Library for the first time. In my own mind, I always celebrate that day," she says. At first, she thought she would spend just a few years in the United States. "I didn't think of it as a permanent thing. It was a gradual process. I thought I would stay two or three years and then go back. I had ten years of indecision." Now she has lived in Minneapolis for more than half her life.

She lived in various apartments in Minneapolis before she finally bought her house, in the pleasant Powderhorn neighborhood, with its big old frame houses and the fast-fading remnants of an earlier Swedish immigrant community. She was befriended by Anna and Axel Ekholm, a Swedish couple who had immigrated to Minnesota years ago. "They made me feel at home here in south Minneapolis. Now that generation of older Swedish immigrants is gone, all within a few years, and immigrants from other countries are moving in."

Still, though she owns a house and has had the same job for more than three decades, she lives in two worlds. However, the lines between them are growing increasingly blurred, she says. A photo taken of her in her early days in Minneapolis is labeled "Minneapolis resident, citizen of the world," an apt description. Her job is one reason for her global focus; her family is another. She is an associate professor at the University of Minnesota and the librarian for the University's Scandinavian collection. She is also the only one in her immediate family to emigrate from Sweden to America.

The University has one of the largest collections of publications in Scandinavian languages in the United States. Other institutions with large collections are Harvard, the University of Wisconsin at Madison, the University of Washington, the Library of Congress and the New York Public Library. As a reference librarian, she is often consulted on issues involving Scandinavia. "I have always enjoyed my job. It has been very stimulating and, because it involves Scandinavia, I have never felt cut off from Sweden. One good thing about my job is that I have been able to meet people from all over the country."

Mariann has been back to Sweden nearly every summer since she left. "I am the unmarried aunt, so I have done a lot of travelling back and forth to see my sisters and their families. I have several nieces and nephews and some of them have been over here, too, which gladdens my heart." The advent of e-mail has made it even easier—not to mention cheaper—to keep in touch with her relatives.

Her pleasant Swedish accent makes it difficult for people to forget where she came from, so she tells them right away that she is Swedish. "I have to get that out of the way the first thing when I meet new people." However, with the presence of so many other Swedish immigrants and descendants of immigrants, Mariann says, "It has always been easier to be Swedish here than in other

The four Tiblin sisters wore identical pink dresses in this photo taken circa 1945. They are, left to right, Ann-Margret, Karin, Ingela and Mariann. Photo by Westberg, Borlänge, Sweden. Photo courtesy of Mariann Tiblin.

places in the United States." In addition to her job, she keeps contact with Swedish and Swedish-American culture through membership in the American Swedish Institute and the Swedish American Historical Society and other organizations. She also makes periodic visits to Ingebretsen Scandinavian Foods, to stock up on crisp breads, flat bread and other Swedish soul food. Nevertheless, she is clear that Minneapolis is not Sweden, as she carefully points out. "I got interested in Swedish-American culture but it is a completely different culture than Swedish culture." Despite her interest and activity in Scandinavian culture, Mariann does draw a line. "I'm not Swedish every day," she says with a laugh. "It's not my whole life. I have several circles that don't always overlap—my church friends, my library friends, my Swedish friends. Someone said, about immigration, that it results not in a divided heart, but in an expanded heart."

Rice Pudding

This is Mariann Tiblin's version of the Swedish Christmas favorite.

Serves Six
2 c. water
1 tsp. salt
1½ tbsp. butter or margarine
1 stick cinnamon
1 c. medium- or short-grain rice
4 c. milk
1 tbsp. sugar
3 eggs, slightly beaten
¾ c. raisins

In a large saucepan, bring water, salt and butter to a boil. Add the rice and cinnamon stick. Cover and cook on low heat for ten minutes. Add the milk and bring to a boil. Cover and place pan over diffused heat (we suggest setting it inside a larger pan filled with an inch or so of water and set over low heat on the stove—a large frying pan works well). The rice will expand in the saucepan. After 30 minutes, remove from heat, remove cinnamon stick and mix sugar into rice. Let rice mixture cool slightly, then mix in the eggs and raisins. Place rice mixture in a greased baking dish and bake at 325–350 degrees for approximately 30 minutes, or until set and lightly browned. Serve with lingonberries or cranberries.

Here's the Beyer family—Emma, left, Bill, Kerstin and Margareta. Bill and Margareta made a real effort to raise their girls bilingually and biculturally. Photo courtesy of Margareta Beyer.

Margareta Jern Beyer and Bill Beyer
Balancing two cultures

Boy meets girl, they fall in love, get married and live happily ever after—so the usual story goes. But what happens when American boy meets Swedish girl and they fall in love and eventually marry? Which country do they live in? What language do they speak? How do they raise their children so that both cultures are honored?

Margareta Jern Beyer and Bill Beyer have worked out their own answers to those questions over their thirty-one year marriage. Margareta, born and raised in Göteborg, Sweden, had a yen to see the United States because she had heard so much about it. "My father was

an engineer for Volvo and he went to Detroit sometimes on business and my step-mother was born in the United States, in Colorado," she said. "My step-grandmother had emigrated to Colorado. She married a Swede there and they moved back to Sweden just before World War I. They thought the United States was the greatest place in the world until I said I was going to move there," laughed Margareta.

The decision to move to the U.S. came four years after Margareta first met Bill Beyer. "I wanted to see the United States and I saw an ad for a four-week summer session for Scandinavian teachers at Luther College [in Decorah, Iowa]. That was in 1966." In 1970 the two were married in the United States. Initially, they chose to live in the U.S., because, as Margareta explained, "I had already bridged the language barrier and I liked Decorah, I felt at home there."

Three years later, they moved to Sweden, partly at Bill's urging. "He just wanted to know Sweden and his attitude was really helpful," said Margareta. In Sweden, Bill not only learned a new language but he learned to know "another" Margareta. "Bill didn't really know who I was until we went to Sweden," said Margareta. "He told me he didn't realize that I could be chatty." After three years in Sweden, they moved back to the United States so Bill could pursue a doctorate in American Studies.

The Beyers live in a charming house in St. Paul, full of light and warmth, with glints of antique copper, Margareta's watercolors of flowers and berries and the smell of good Swedish coffee. Margareta teaches reading to first- and second-graders who have had trouble mastering it at Phalen Lake Elementary School in St. Paul, and Bill is an executive with a software company.

The Beyers' two children—Kerstin, 25, and Emma, 21—are grown and far away, Kerstin teaching English in Japan and Emma studying at the University of Puget Sound in Washington state. Kerstin recently sent her parents an e-mail saying "All my friends are rushing around the world as adults to learn more languages. I thank you both for making sure Emma and I learned both Swedish and English. I may have been embarrassed in the second grade, but I now know how lucky I am.'"

Rearing the children bilingually was a conscious effort for the Beyers. "When the girls were little, until they started having friends in, I always spoke Swedish to them. I sang Swedish lullabies to them and taught them Swedish songs. We had Swedish books and tapes, too.

For years our oldest daughter would fall asleep listening to Astrid Lindgren reading *Madicken*. All of this really added to their picking up the Swedish culture and language," said Margareta.

The Beyers made many trips to Sweden during summers and both girls spent one semester in Swedish high schools and attended summer confirmation camp in Sweden. Later, Kerstin took a year off from her studies at Vassar College to go to a folk high school in Sweden. "She's a real world citizen, always wanting to travel and see other countries," said Margareta.

The Beyers' younger daughter, Emma, had more questions about her cultural identity, according to Margareta. "Sweden has been more important for Emma. She felt that, in this country, she wasn't really American, and in Sweden, she wasn't really Swedish, so she decided to spend her junior year in Stockholm and now she feels she is Swedish when she goes to Sweden."

Emma said, "Spending a year in Sweden made me feel more comfortable about my dual identities. Living with two cultures validated both and I didn't have to choose one over the other. It also means I don't have to move to Greenland," she added with a laugh, "That's what I thought when I was little, because Greenland is in between Sweden and America."

Margareta balances the two cultures adroitly in her own life, even to alternating Swedish and American recipes. "I do enjoy living here and I do enjoy my American friends who are open to other cultures and ideas, but I also like to get together with my Swedish friends because I don't have to explain myself. I like that I have both cultures," said Margareta. "I like to pick the best of both societies."

Sjömansbiff

(sailor's beef)

This is Margareta Beyer's recipe for this traditional hearty dish. Margareta's recipe, along with some of the others in this book, are also collected in *Var Så God,* published by the American Swedish Institute in 1980.

Serves four.
3 medium onions, sliced
2 tbsp. butter or margarine
1 lb. beef (round or rump steak), cut in thin strips
2–3 tsp. salt
¼ tsp. white pepper (or a little less black pepper)
10–12 small potatoes (about 2 lb.), peeled and sliced
2 c. beer (or bouillon or 1 bottle beer plus ⅔ c. water)

In a frying pan, brown onions in butter. Remove onions from pan and add the meat. Brown the meat and add salt and pepper. Layer potatoes, onions and meat in a pot, sprinkling a little salt over the potatoes. Rinse out frying pan with the liquid (beer, etc) and pour over ingredients in the pot. Cover and cook slowly for ¾ to 1 hour, either on top of the stove or in the oven at 375 degrees, until potatoes are soft and meat is tender. Serve from the pot, with a green salad or grated carrots.

This is one of the songs Margareta sang to her daughters when they were young. It is a traditional Swedish song.

Vem kan segla förutan vind

Vem kan segla förutan vind
vem kan ro utan åror?
Vem kan skiljas från vännen sin
utan att fälla tårar?

Jag kan segla förutan vind
jag kan ro utan åror
Men ej skiljas från vännen min
utan att fälla tårar.

(translation—Anne Gillespie Lewis)

Who can sail without wind,
who can row without oars?
Who can part from a friend
without letting tears fall?

I can sail without wind,
I can row without oars
But I can never part from a friend
without letting tears fall

Annie Robertson, right, also known as Inga Svensson, was a cook in the household of Alexander Ramsey. She is shown with Ramsey's granddaughter, Laura Furness, circa 1905. Photo courtesy of the Minnesota Historical Society.

Chapter Four

Swedes at Work

The Swedes developed a reputation as hard working. Early in the immigration period, many of the newcomers worked with their hands. The men were often carpenters or worked in other aspects of the building trades or for the creameries. The young women who worked were most often domestics or factory workers. As is always the case, some did very well financially. Some creameries in the Twin Cities were owned by Swedes and some of the largest construction companies were also started by Swedish-Americans. One of Minnesota's most successful men, the late Curt Carlson, who built a travel and hospitality mega-business, was a Swedish-American.

As the immigrants and their descendants became educated, their occupations changed. Below are several stories of men and women who worked for a living in the Twin Cities.

As with any group of new immigrants, the Swedes encountered prejudice from those who had come before them. They weren't always well-accepted by the entrenched residents and as late as a 1923 history of Minneapolis, the Scandinavians seemed to be regarded by the author as being apart from the mainstream.[1]

Annie Robertson
"All rests with Annie the cook."

The old photo on page 60 shows a pretty young woman, with big eyes—probably blue—dark hair pulled back into a neat bun and a waist that looks very small to the twenty-first century eye. She looks to be in her twenties in the formal black-and-white portrait that shows her in a smart dark dress with a long row of tiny buttons down the front, watch tucked neatly in her pocket. Perhaps she had the photo taken for her sweetheart, who preceded her to the United States. The picture is reported to be of Inga Svensson and she was Swedish. She had a brother and sisters, but we don't know where she was born in Sweden.

Now look at the photo on page 62. See the elderly woman on the left, white-haired and smiling slightly? That is Annie Robertson, who was the cook for Alexander Ramsey—Minnesota's first territorial governor—and his family for 37 years, from 1889 to 1926. The governor was a gourmand, perhaps glutton is a more apt description, and Annie the cook was very important to his household. He often mentioned her in his journal and she was so much a part of the life of the family that her funeral was held at the Ramsey House, which is now one of the Minnesota Historical Society's sites.

Compare the two photos: the set of the shoulders is similar in both women and the old lady's waist, while not as tidy as the young girl's, is definitely under control. Why are we doing this? Haven't you guessed? Inga and Annie were one and the same person, although the

This is reportedly an 1873 photo of Annie Robertson, a Swedish immigrant who cooked for the Alexander Ramsey family. Palmquist & Jurgens photo, courtesy of the Minnesota Historical Society.

Jennie Olstad Haroldsen, who worked as a maid at the Ramsey House early in the twentieth century, was interviewed and taped by her son and daughter in 1975. During the interview, her daughter said to her, "I understand the cook was real good and kind to you."

Her mother replied: "Uh-huh, she was so nice, she couldn't be nasty. She was old Swedish cook . . . She came from Sweden . . . That boy that she was going to marry was here before and when she came she found out he had already married somebody so she got this cooking job and she learned cooking in Sweden. How old she was when she come over I don't know but she wasn't very young when I was there and she worked there twenty years already. And then she said that boy she was going to get married to, his wife died and then he came and he wanted to marry her and she said no."[2]

So—it was an old story: Inga/Annie was jilted and had to earn her living. Instead of running her own household, she was a big factor in running the Ramsey House. The governor's wife had died five years before Annie came to work there in 1889. The lady of the house was Ramsey's daughter, Marion Furness, who had been left on her own with three children—Anita, Laura and Alexander Ramsey Furness, whom the family called Ramsey. The daughters never married and lived in the house until they died, Laura in 1959 and Anita in 1964. The house was donated to the Historical Society. Thus, many of the furnishings have survived intact.

reason for her changing her name remains obscure. According to a report made years later by another servant in the Ramsey household, Inga came to the United States expecting to get married.

Visitors to the house can see the kitchen where Annie and her helpers worked. The kitchen is furnished with some of the utensils Annie probably used. A historical society employee now plays the part of the cook when people tour the house and she occasionally hands out fresh-baked cookies.

Although the Ramseys never wrote anything nasty about Annie and apparently considered her a loyal fixture in the house, there were hints by other servants interviewed later that there was a definite "Upstairs, Downstairs" mentality operating. Carlotte Wickstrom Carlson, who worked at the house from the fall of 1913 until the following May, described a scene in the kitchen when Mrs. Furness, who had been out calling on friends, came in—probably unexpectedly—through the back door into the kitchen.

". . . you know we had coffee;" Carlson told the interviewers who were taping her memories. "we weren't supposed to have coffee between times, but the cook cooked for us; she cooked [apparently she referred to Annie making coffee, ed.] in the oven so it wasn't going to smell, and I know one time when she [Mrs. Furness] came in she just (Carlson made an inhaling noise) like that when she walked through, you know, but she didn't say anything and Anna [Annie] said, 'I was going to ask her whether she wanted a cup of coffee.' (followed by the sound of laughter on the tape). Oh dear, but she [Annie] was nice."[3]

So, Annie had a sense of humor, it seems. She also had friends in when the Ramsey family was gone, according to Eileen DeWald, of South St. Paul, Minnesota. Mrs. DeWald said that her grandmother, Ida Theresa Swanson Larson, who was also a Swedish immigrant and belonged to the same church as Annie did, was a guest for Sunday dinner on several occasions when Laura and Anita Furness were spending summers on Cape Cod. Mrs. DeWald's mother, Charlotte Larson Lorch, also was

at the dinners.[4] Like most servants of that era, Annie didn't get much time off, but she may have been a regular churchgoer. The Ramseys gave their servants time off for church on Sunday morning and most also had every other Sunday off although it seems clear from the governor's journal that the cook always prepared Sunday dinner. Annie was a long-time member of First Lutheran Church, the oldest Lutheran church in either Minneapolis or St. Paul. The church is located on the east side of St. Paul, adjacent to Swede Hollow, the first Swedish neighborhood in the Twin Cities, about four miles round trip from Ramsey House, which is located in the Irvine Park area west of downtown. An earlier church building was closer to downtown, but still more than a three-mile round trip from the house. Gov. Ramsey drove earlier servants to church, and it is possible that Annie sometimes had a ride to church. At church, Annie became Inga (or sometimes Ingrid) again. She is listed in several church directories, which were published every few years, as Ingrid or Inga Swenson—with her last name spelled in a couple of variations—living at 265 S. Exchange St., the Ramsey residence.

Over the years, many other Swedes worked for the Ramseys, including John Pommer, who was the gardener, according to Dana Heimark, assistant site manager at the Ramsey House. Pommer also assisted the elderly Gov. Ramsey with his monthly bath, clipped his toenails and dunned farmers for their rent money, Dana said. He even took Ramsey's grandchildren to the circus, as noted in the governor's journal entry of Sept. 10, 1890.[5] In 1880, nine years before Annie started as cook, the 1880 census shows four servants at the Ramsey House, all from Sweden.[6]

Annie Robertson, also known as Inga Svensson, is at left in this group photo—Photo courtesy of the Minnesota Historical Society.

The Ramseys often referred to Annie in letters and it was common for them to end letters to other family members with greetings to or from Annie. References to her within the bodies of the letters were often brief. The original spelling is given here. On July 20, 1894, Marion Furness wrote to Anita and Ramsey, and included the line "Minnie [apparently another servant] came home last evening . . . and Annie leaves tomorrow for a week."[7]

The family seemed to think highly of Annie, whom they called by the honorific "Mrs.," though she was never married. In a letter from Ramsey Furness to his sister, Anita, on Sept. 25, 1894, he writes: "We got a telegram last night from Mama saying that you had arrived safely in London, and so I immediately went up and told Mrs. Robertson."[8]

Annie was well aware of the family's likes and dislikes. Mrs. Furness wrote to her daughter, Anita, on Jan. 20, 1895, "Annie the other day when she was making ginger snaps, said, "Miss Nita liked these so."[9]

Alexander Ramsey seemed inordinately fond of his food. In his journal entry of August 16, 1900, he writes: "A fisherman who regularly attends the fresh fish market on Wabasha bridge . . . brought a medium sized snapping turtle of which to my surprise he asked only fourteen cents! Now all rests with Annie the cook!"[10]

Two days later, on August 18, he wrote, "Our turtle brot on the table at lunch."[11]

Food was apparently the subject of much discussion with the Ramseys. Writing to his daughter on March 7, 1891, he says: "I left the question for to-morrow dinner to a vote at the table & it was [conceded] that the dish should be rost-beef. Today it is to be pot-pie & yesterday we had a boiled dinner ¾ of which was consumed by the bells & beax of the kitchen."[12]

To his daughter on March 15, 1891, he wrote "We have some very interesting discussions as to what from day to day the dinner is to be & today we are to be content with roast turkey."[13]

Annie and her assistants produced prodigious amounts of food for lunches and parties. Mrs. Furness wrote her daughter Anita on June 9, 1895 that she had invited 68 people to lunch (though some declined) and planned to have "bouillon—Caviar Sandwiches + radishes, Chicken croquettes, peas + Saratoga potatoes— Stuffed Tomatoe salad with cheese crackers—Ice cream + frozen Strawberries + Cake—Coffee."[14]

In a letter to Anita on June 16, 1895, she wrote: "My luncheon on Wednesday was an unqualified success . . . I think I gave you the menu in my last letter. I only substituted lobster a la Newburg with cucumber sandwiches for the caviar & radishes. Everything was deliciously cooked and nicely served . . . There were fifty there altogether, and of course the rooms were not all crowded."[15]

In addition to the cooking, Annie did at least some of the shopping and also did much of the preserving. "Annie has been pressing peaches and quincey and making pickles—sour and sweet," Alexander Ramsey wrote to his daughter on October 3, 1894.[16]

Mrs. Furness and her daughters seem to have made a little attempt at cooking, mainly when Annie or the others were out. In a July 4, 1899, letter to Laura, Mrs. Furness writes, "Now I must 'get' tea Christine & Annie being both out."[17] In a letter to Anita on December 15, 1895, she wrote: "Last Sunday evening Wade Hampton dropped in to Tea. Annie had gone out so we had to cook our own meal. It was very simple, however, eggs, scrambled in the chafing dish, and I made him do the stirring."[18]

Mrs. Furness seems to have helped Annie a bit, too. In a letter from Marion Furness to her daughter Laura on October 21, 1900, she writes, "I have been sewing hard this morning helping Annie make two pillows for 'dose bebbies,' who are to be baptized this afternoon."[19]

The cooking, the preserving and the coddling of the Ramsey and Furness families went on year after year, decade after decade. Annie apparently saved most of her salary and when she died at the age of 73, in 1926, she had more than $7,000 in the bank.[20] Her estate was divided among her brother, her surviving sisters in Sweden and several nephews.[21] Her funeral was held at the Ramsey House and she is buried in Union Cemetery, on the east side of St. Paul. Unlike most immigrants of the time, her passing was noted with a news obituary in the *St. Paul Pioneer Press* on April 20, 1926. The paper gave a laudatory, if somewhat naïve view of her as a servant:

"To her and her really able kind, the kitchen of a house was no mere alcove for the hasty assembling of hastily consumed meals. It was an important and self-respecting department, without the thoroughgoing co-operation of which there could be no real domestic welfare. And, for 37 years she supplied such co-operation with her heart and her hands.

Her skill had a vital share in the hospitality, formal and informal, for which the house has been famous for these many years.

She took keen pleasure in noting the preferences of various guests for special dishes, and never failed to remember them, however long it might be between visits.

For she was one of the old-fashioned servants who chose to identify themselves with the interests of the family they served, and looked upon its fortunes and misfortunes as their own."[22]

Ginger Snaps

These ginger snaps, probably similar to the ones Annie Robertson made when she was the cook at the Ramsey House, are still made and sometimes given to visitors at the Ramsey House in St. Paul.

¾ c. unsalted butter
¾ c. lard or solid shortening
2 c. sugar
2 eggs
½ c. molasses
¼ tsp. salt
2 tsp. baking soda
2 tsp. cinnamon
2 tsp. ginger
½ tsp. cloves
4 c. flour
sugar for rolling cookies in

In a large bowl, cream butter and lard or shortening. Add 2 cups sugar and beat until fluffy. Beat in eggs one at a time. Add molasses. Stir in salt, baking soda, cinnamon, ginger and cloves. Stir in flour one cup at a time. Chill cookie dough one hour. Form the dough into one-inch balls and roll each in sugar. Place two inches apart on cookie sheet and bake in a preheated oven at 375 degrees for 12–15 minutes. Allow cookies to cool 3–4 minutes before removing from cookie sheet. These cookies will lose their crispness in damp, humid weather.

Annie the cook, Lizzie the nursemaid and thousands of others

Annie Robertson/Inga Svensson was just one of the many Swedish servants at the Alexander Ramsey house during the late nineteenth and early twentieth centuries. Dana Heimark, assistant site manager at Ramsey House, said, "By the 1870s, probably more than half were Swedish. It's hard to say whether they were hired because they were Swedish or whether the Swedish servants who were already there encouraged them to apply."

Usually, the Ramsey household had four servants— the cook, the gardener, an upstairs servant and a downstairs servant, according to Dana. When Ramsey's three grandchildren lived in the house, there were two additional servants—a nursemaid and a governess. When large parties or dinners were scheduled, the Ramseys borrowed servants from their friends for the event.

"The servants were really under-appreciated," said Dana. "They made the household operate." Alexander Ramsey, Minnesota's first territorial governor, reportedly came from a working class background—his father was a blacksmith and his mother was said to be a laundress— and he seemed to treat the servants better than his daughter or granddaughters, according to remarks in their letters and in Ramsey's journal, Dana said. "Mister Ramsey's background may have influenced his handling of the servants," she added.

Anita Furness, Ramsey's granddaughter, had a cook working for her until her death in 1964, long after most wealthy families had to do their own cooking. Anita and her sister, Laura, apparently did not do much cooking. In an oral history recorded on October 11, 1991, Jenny Walen, who worked as a cook for the household from 1937 to the middle of 1939, told the interviewer that they never cooked. "Once they asked me to fix them a hot dish of some kind. I can't remember what it was, but Miss Laura asked me to show her how to turn on the gas oven in the evening when she would need it. I showed her, and the next morning she came in and she had her eyebrows singed off because she had let the gas on too long and lit the end of the oven."[23]

Many immigrants and daughters of immigrants staffed the big houses in Minneapolis and St. Paul. Many families with Scandinavian ancestry, including my own, have a grandmother or other relative who worked as a servant. My grandmother, Melissa ("Lizzie") Caroline Petersen Anderson, worked as a nursemaid for a wealthy family who lived on Summit Avenue in St. Paul. My mother said Granny went to work, from her home in Red Wing, Minnesota, when she was 15 years old. It would have been in the same time period Annie Robertson worked as a cook for the Ramseys. Granny spoke her own mind even at that early age and she later told my mother about one occasion when the lady of the house was expecting company and the cook was apparently out. Her boss told my grandmother that she wanted to make coffee for the visitors but that she didn't know how. Perhaps she thought my grandmother would then offer to make the coffee for her. No such luck. Granny, my mother reported, said: "Why, I would be ashamed to admit that I didn't know how to make coffee" and marched the woman into her own kitchen and showed her how.

I have no idea how much Granny made at that time late in the nineteenth century or very early in the twentieth, but a report by a state agency in the late 1880s tells many details—good and bad—about domestic servants.

Melissa Caroline Petersen Anderson, the author's grandmother who was a nursemaid to a wealthy family on Summit Avenue, is second from left in the front row. Her hair, which appears white in the photo, was actually platinum blonde. Her sister Agnes, is at left in the front row. Their parents are also pictured. This was the first meeting of the Ladies Aid Society at St. Paul's Lutheran Church in Red Wing, Minnesota, in 1897 or 1898. Photo courtesy of Jean Ross.

The report, the first in a series, is titled *Biennial report of the Bureau of Labor Statistics of the State of Minnesota for the two years ending 1887–1888.*[24]

It tells the average weekly wage for women workers in a variety of occupations. Some samples: hotel cooks, $4.37; buttonhole makers in boot and shoe factories, $7.05; sewers in fur businesses, $5.61; candy wrappers, $4.10; shirt makers, $3.66; dish washers in restaurants $3.83; and common help in hotels, $2.25.[25] Annie Robertson, Dana said, probably made about $17 per month, with room and board included.

The report goes into great detail, with remarks from women who were domestics, those who were employed in other businesses, staff of employment agencies, and even from employers. Those who chose to work in other jobs were often very dismissive of domestic work. A book-bindery employee said, "I would not do housework under any consideration. In the first place, I would not be anyone's servant. In the second place, I am not obliged to. In the third place, girls, as a rule, are not treated properly. I know a woman who compels her girls to eat in the back shed."[26]

A shirtmaker said, "My objection to housework is that in many places a hired girl is much less than a dog; all hours are working hours: never any extra pay for any kind of extra work. Have had many years of personal experience at housework."[27]

Domestic workers often painted a gloomy picture of their jobs: "Won't average more than one hour's spare time each day. Sometimes I have a chance to go to church Sundays at 6 A.M." said one.[28]

Some were a little more philosophical: "Sometimes the treatment is good; sometimes it is bad," said one worker.[29]

Another echoed this in more detail: "I worked in a place three months where I had to get up at five o'clock A.M. and work until 9:30 P.M. It nearly killed me. Then I worked in another place for nine months, and was well treated. Have had three and a half years experience at family work, and I do not want any more family places."[30]

The report itself was not above editorializing, prefacing one domestic's comments with the notation: "From a girl of fifteen years experience at all kinds of general housework—exceptionally intelligent and sensible." This "girl" said, "I think that about half the people who hire help do not treat them properly. In some places the treatment is shameful. I believe that an organization for domestics would do a great deal of good."[31]

The staff at employment agencies were frank in their opinions also. One said, "Two thirds of the girls at present engaged in housework are Skandinavians [sic]. Of these I should say that two thirds are Swedes, and one-third Norwegians. . . . For cooking and waiting on table the Irish girls are considered the best. For general housework the Germans and Norwegians. There are a great many good Swede girls, but they are not considered so cleanly as other nationalities; and not so much sought for. Nearly all the girls are pretty well educated in their own language . . ."[32]

The same person continued: "House girls usually commence at 6 A.M. They generally have from one to two hours in the afternoon and evening [off], and afternoons Thursdays and Sundays. I think that about five per cent of those people who hire help are utterly unfit for any one to work for. The average wages are from $2.50 to $3.50 per week for general housework . . . Wages are not as high this year (1888) except for very competent help; they are on an average twenty-five per cent less this year than last."[33]

Another employment office worker said, ". . . There is one characteristic common to the Norwegians, Danes and Germans. They are more stable in their habits, not wishing to change places only as seldom as possible. The Swedes, on the other hand, while somewhat more versatile, are more fickle and care less for steady employment. We find place for fully 3,000 girls every year from the Minneapolis office, and an equal number from the St. Paul office. The business is constantly increasing. I should think that there were fully 8,000 girls employed in this city. Should say that they worked ten hours a day on an average.

The ordinary wages in private families are $2.50 and $3.00 per week. That is the rule. The new comers and inexperienced girls get $2.00 until they can speak English—that is for the first month. They learn English in five or six weeks so that they can understand the names of all the things they have to deal with in the house; they then get $2.50 and $3.00. Girls who have had experience and are superior in housework get $3.50 to $5.00 per week."[34]

Even well-meaning employers could sound snobbish and patronizing as well, as shown in this letter, dated Aug. 22, 1888: "In reply to your inquiries in regard to the girls who do our housework, I will say: First, that there are all varieties of girls who seek such employment, the majority of them untrained and ignorant of their business. They are, nearly all, foreigners, by birth or parentage, many, perhaps the largest number, from Scandinavia. They come here utterly ignorant of our ways, knew nothing of cooking, cannot make a bed properly and have no skill even in sweeping and dusting. Some have only acquired a few words of our language, but nearly all of them can say 'tree dolla,' which is their usual demand for a week's work . . . The training of such girls is very wearing on the mistress of the house and not very many have the patience and forbearance necessary for the task; but those who persevere in teaching them faithfully and kindly are amply rewarded . . . The Scandinavians are generally reliable and faithful, thrifty and economical and very desirous to get as high wages as possible."[35]

The writer continues with suggestions for improving the situation, including having a training school to teach girls housework and having employers provide sitting rooms for the girls, with "their work table, comfortable chairs, perhaps some books and pictures, a blooming plant or something to gratify their taste for beautiful things. This would foster their self respect and prevent much of the running on the streets in the evening with associates, and meeting those who lie in wait for unwary girls."[36]

She does add that much of the friction is due to employers: "Doubtless much of the trouble . . . is owing to the employers, who are often exacting, overbearing and unkind, but we will hope that they too are learning lessons as to their duties to their domestics."[37]

Of course, the "trouble" eventually took care of itself as the "girls," once in such great supply, married and set up their own households. Soon the flow of immigrants slowed and the wealthy women had to learn to make their own beds and cook their own meals.

Axel Ohman was a sturdy twelve-year-old in Tibble, Dalarna, Sweden, when this photo was taken. He was already working hard. Photo courtesy of Axel Ohman.

Axel Ohman
He built half of Minneapolis

Axel Ohman is often introduced as "the man who built half of Minneapolis." Though he turned 96 in June of 2001, Axel still has sharp memories of his building projects and points them out to his wife, Gudrun ("Goody") and other people when he is out riding along the streets of his adopted city. Axel's buildings spanned several generations. He worked on the 32-story Foshay Tower in downtown Minneapolis, which was for many years the tallest building in the area. It was finished in 1929 and the gala opening celebrated by a special tune, written and performed by the legendary John Phillip Sousa and his band.

A legion of other projects include: the IDS Center, spiritual successor to the Foshay as the city's tallest building; the Prudential building; Southdale Shopping Mall, which was the first covered shopping center in the United States; an addition to the St. Paul post office; the original Mount Olivet Lutheran Church on 50th Street in south Minneapolis and the current church, just across the street from the first church; the Mayo building at the University of Minnesota; the much lamented Metropolitan Stadium in Bloomington, where the Minnesota Twins got their start; and its counterpart, the temple-like home for the North Stars hockey team, which decamped for Texas, leaving the sturdy building standing forlorn. "That hockey rink was so well-built that they had to dynamite it twice before it came down," said Goody Ohman.

In addition to the big buildings, Axel built many homes in the Twin Cities, including his own. Inside his stone house in south Minneapolis are many examples of his brickwork, including fireplaces and a handsome black brick stove.

Ohman's story is the American dream come true. He started life in the community of Tibble, near Leksand in the province of Dalarna. By the time he was ten years old, he was working ten hours a day in summer helping

Axel Ohman, at right, learned the masonry trade after he came to the United States. Later, he laid the stone for his house in south Minneapolis. Photo courtesy of Axel Ohman.

in a vegetable garden. He moved on to work in a sawmill and then decided to emigrate to the U.S. with his buddy, Alvin Lundell, who now lives in Bloomington, a Minneapolis suburb. The "boys" have remained friends to this day. "Oh, I was very ambitious," said Axel. "My uncle loaned me the money to come and I was very happy to get here. I celebrated my 17th birthday here."

Many birthdays have passed since he came to Minnesota. In the early years, he made a brief detour to Chicago but came back for the social life, taking a pay cut to do so. "Money isn't everything," he said. Axel went to school to learn English and also took blueprint reading and estimating for two years at Dunwoody Institute in addition to working full-time, sometimes seven days a week. In his spare time, he played soccer and loved to go to dances. He remembers, in vivid de-

tail, what his early life was like, who he worked for as a bricklayer and even what he was paid for each job. "I just loved laying brick," he said. He didn't work for others for long. When he was just 22, he was taken in as a partner and he later formed his own construction company. He ran it for decades before selling in 1976. It has since changed hands twice but is still called Axel H. Ohman, Inc.

One of his last big jobs was building Ancker Hospital in St. Paul. "That was one I was very proud of," said Axel. It was a challenge as part of it was round, so that nurses could easily see all the patients from a central station.

As he grew older, Axel reaped many honors, but he also had sadness in his life. His only child, Dennis Holger Ohman, died in his early twenties. In the lower level of his house, Axel has a beautiful cabinet dedicated to his son's memory. It is filled with memorabilia from Dennis' short life.

Axel Ohman was proud of his first automobile, a 1924 Ford Coupe. Photo courtesy of Axel Ohman.

Axel Ohman, center, was the second person to be named "Swede of the Year" at the annual Svenskarnas Dag *celebration at Minnehaha Park, in 1961. Entrepreneur Curt Carlson, left, and Minneapolis Fire Chief Rey Malmquist, were given the accolade in other years. Photo courtesy of Axel Ohman.*

Although he has been in the United States for much longer than he lived in Sweden, he is obviously proud of his roots. One room in his house is decorated with paintings done in the *dala* style of painting popularized in the province of Dalarna where he was born. He has been an active member of many Swedish-American groups, including the American Swedish Institute. He was chosen "Swede of the Year" at the *Svenskarnas Dag* celebration in 1961. Although his health is not so good now, he tries to get to the monthly meetings of the *Dalaförening*, a group formed mostly of people who have an attachment to the province of Dalarna.

Axel has not forgotten Sweden and Sweden has remembered him: he was awarded a medal by the king of Sweden. "That was the old king, you know," said Axel,

meaning Gustaf VI Adolf. Axel, in turn, gave the king a peace pipe from Minnesota. At the ceremony, in Sweden, the king was talking to Axel in Swedish. "Then he asked Goody where she was from and she said Montana and he switched to English. I think he was more interested in her than in me," Axel said jokingly.

A generous man as well as astute businessman, Axel has helped raise money to build an auditorium onto the building that is the American Swedish Institute and he donated funds to his hometown of Tibble for a community center.

Axel Ohman and a friend pose for the camera. Axel and many other young Swedish immigrants belonged to lodges that provided them with a meeting place where they could speak Swedish, meet others and dance. Photo courtesy of Axel Ohman.

Axel Ohman's masonry and concrete contracting business was at its busiest during the fifties and sixties. Here Axel is at left, with his employees standing by company trucks. He sold the business in 1976. Nordin Studio photo, courtesy of Axel Ohman.

This poem, sung to the tune of *T'was on the Isle of Capri* was a rousing tribute to Axel Ohman on his eightieth birthday, June 29, 1985.

Det var en dalmas, som for ut i världen,
att pröva lyckan på främmande strand,
men se varhelst han nu än ställde färden
han ej glömde sitt fädernesland.

refrain:
Allting blev ej bara lycka,
sorger fick han pröva på,
Men han hade lärt att tycka
om att jobba hårt också

Translation (Anne Gillespie Lewis):
"There was a Dala boy who set out in the world
to try his luck on a foreign shore
but no matter how far he has journeyed
he never forgot his fatherland."

Refrain:
"Not only good things happened
sorrow also tested him
but he learned to love working hard, too."

Victor Fridlund, center, is flanked by his daughter, Mildred Pettit, at left, and daughter-in-law, Lindy Fridlund. Mildred's daughter, Marilyn Pettit Brakke, is in the baby buggy. Photo courtesy of Marilyn Brakke.

Victor Fridlund
A visit with Uncle Vic

Marilyn Brakke's Uncle Vic—her mother's brother—lives with his wife, Lindy, in a big, comfortable house in Edina. Vic Fridlund and his dad, also named Victor Fridlund, built the house in 1936. It has a handsome carved fireplace mantel and rich oak woodwork and paneling salvaged from a house that was demolished down by the Mississippi River. "Little Vic"—which people used to call him to distinguish him from his dad, "Big Vic"—has lived in it ever since. "I've only lived in two houses since I was born—this one and the house on Dupont." He and Lindy raised their three kids in the Edina house and pictures of the kids and the grandchildren are everywhere in the living room. Their son Wayne, also an independent builder—like his father and grandfather before him—lives in the house next to the Fridlunds.

Uncle Vic is 87 now and a little stooped. In his prime,

he was six-foot, two-inches tall, but he's lost a few inches. He quit working as a builder when he was about 80, but continued to scramble up and down ladders. "Last year I could still climb a ladder, but not now." Over lunch, he and Lindy reminisced with Marilyn about their family, particularly about "Big Vic," who came from Småland, Sweden, when he was 19 years old. No one seems to know any details of why he immigrated or what it was like for him at home in Sweden, except that his father was a cabinet maker. "He never mentioned anything about Sweden and he never went back. He was always worried about his sisters here, though," said Vic. Four of his sisters followed him to the United States, one by one, though a sister and a brother and his parents remained in Sweden.

Marilyn recalls her mother saying that Big Vic sat in a chair when he was in his 80s and had tears in his eyes because he had never written home to his mother, though his wife wrote to her. Little Vic looks skeptical as he tells this, shaking his head slightly. "Well, your mother was always emotional, always boo-hooing" he says to Marilyn. "She would cry at the movies. One time she cried at a Charlie Chaplin movie when Charlie boiled his shoe because he didn't have anything else to eat." Marilyn chuckles a little and responds, "Well, I can picture her standing in front of him and saying, 'Aren't you sorry you didn't write to your mother?'"

Big Vic didn't teach his kids Swedish, although Little Vic learned a few words—some of them naughty ones—from the Swedish carpenters he worked with. None of Big Vic's kids speak Swedish, either, and neither does Marilyn. Only two things tie Little Vic to Sweden—food and a photograph. At Christmas, the Fridlunds may have rice pudding, but most will pass on the *lutfisk*. "My dad loved that stuff [*lutfisk*]. He could eat it like crazy," says Little Vic. The other echo of Sweden is the beautiful tinted photo of the farmstead in Småland that hangs on the wall in the Fridlunds' porch. Big Vic did belong to the Swedish Brothers, an insurance organization, but he didn't bother to go to *Svenskarnas Dag*, the annual midsummer gathering of Swedes and Swedish-Americans at Minnehaha Falls. His son doesn't feel sentimental about his heritage, either. "I never thought of it as anything special. I just took what I got." Some of his cousins have visited relations in Sweden and some of the Swedes have also come to Minnesota in turn. Little Vic shrugs his shoulders; delving into his heritage just doesn't interest him much.

Mabel Fridlund, whose parents were from Sweden, was born in a sod house in what is now Milbank, South Dakota, in 1885. Though she was Swedish on both her mother's and father's side, her maiden name was Lincoln. Another niece of Uncle Vic's, Polly Thill, later explained how she got the name. Polly says that when her great-grandfather, whose last name was originally Lingon, came through customs, the customs agent couldn't understand his name. When he repeated it, according to Polly, the man said, "Oh, Lincoln—like the president." "Why, he was a good man," the newcomer replied, and "Lincoln" he became. Mabel's family later moved to Minneapolis, where her father continued to work as a stonemason. He later joined his son-in-law in building many houses, including the foundation of the house that Big Vic and Mabel Fridlund lived in for so many years at 4943 Dupont Avenue South. Early in his career as a builder, Big Vic built Lynnhurst Congregational Church at 45th and Colfax South and he and Mabel became charter members of the church. Their children would later be married there. Their son Victor was born there in 1914 and his sister—Marilyn's mother, Mildred—was born in 1912. Their older brother

"Little Vic" (Victor Fridlund Jr.) and his wife, Lindy, were married in Lynnhurst Congregational Church in Minneapolis. His father built the church. Photo courtesy of Marilyn Brakke.

Harold—Polly's father—was born in 1906. When the kids were young, the whole family showed up for Saturday night dances.

Little Vic's days working as a builder with his dad and his crew are still very vivid in his memory. "When I was little, I'd be upset with my mother because she didn't wake me up to go to work with my dad on Saturdays."

He started pretty young, though, helping out his dad when he was eight or nine. "At thirteen, I was up on the roof shingling. I was always hanging out, trying to learn how things were done. I learned a lot from 'Black Gus' [a black-haired Swede; there was also a blond "Sandy Gus"]. He was an alcoholic, but he was an excellent carpenter. He'd be drinking on weekends and sometimes we had to go look for him. He lived in a place on Cedar Avenue, near Seven Corners. Maybe Tuesday morning he'd show up. My dad never got mad at him. I kept in touch with him for several years. He used to come out to our house on the streetcar. One weekend he got hit by a car and I went to visit him in the hospital. He still lived down there on Cedar."

"Black Gus" was one of a crew of eight or nine who worked for Big Vic building houses. There were usually two or three carpenters in the bunch, a cement man, a bricklayer and some others, depending on what the job was. "They all did everything," says Little Vic. "My dad had his own business and he would be called by architects and he would get the plans and build the house. They sometimes worked up to a year on one house, it wasn't like today. I was 21 when I started taking over the physical work and my dad did the other things." Mabel Fridlund kept the books for the business and brought the men hot lunches when they worked late.

The Fridlund crew stuck together, Little Vic says. "They'd help each other out if something was wrong. Once a crank on a Model T Ford backfired and a painter broke his wrist and of course he couldn't paint with a broken wrist so they had a big party for him and brought food and had a dance in the firehouse on 42nd and Chicago. They would help each other out until they got over the problem."

Little Vic left the business during World War II, when he served with the Army Engineers in Iran. He spent three years there building railroad stations, roads, bridges, and docks so that the United States could ship supplies "through the back door" into Russia. "If it hadn't been for that supply line, Germany would have overrun Russia," he says.

The building business, which had been in the doldrums during the Depression, picked up when the war ended. "After the war, it went crazy." Little Vic has long ago lost count of the houses he and his dad built, but he knows it is at least a hundred. All sturdy and strong—like the men who built them. It is left to Lindy to deliver an impromptu eulogy for her father-in-law, Big Vic: "He was a great, great man. To come from another country with no education and nobody to guide him and to do all that. We're very proud of him."

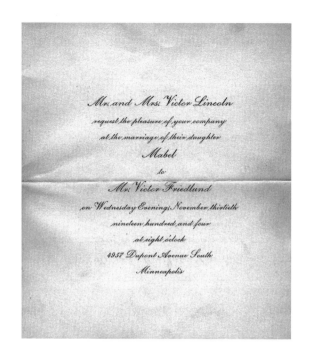

Mr. and Mrs. Victor Lincoln
request the pleasure of your company
at the marriage of their daughter
Mabel
to
Mr. Victor Fridlund
on Wednesday Evening, November thirtieth
nineteen hundred and four
at eight o'clock
4957 Dupont Avenue South
Minneapolis

Top left, Mabel Lincoln Fridlund's crush on "Big Vic" led to their later marriage. Top right, Mabel Lincoln and Vic Fridlund's wedding invitation. Below right, Victor and Mabel Fridlund lived many happy years together. Their granddaughter, Marilyn Brakke, said "Grandma and Grandpa Frid were low-key, quiet, un-assuming, pleasant, hard-working people who loved to drink coffee and dunk cinnamon toast late at night or make root beer floats on hot summer evenings." Photos courtesy of Marilyn Brakke.

How Big Vic and Mabel Met

Polly Thill loves to tell the story of her grandparents' meeting and marriage. According to Polly, when Mabel Lincoln Fridlund was just a little, red-haired girl, her dad hired Victor Fridlund, a young Swedish immigrant, to help him build his house on Dupont Avenue South in Minneapolis. Mabel's dad—also from Sweden—was a stonemason and Vic Fridlund was a carpenter. Dupont Avenue was practically countryside at that time and Mabel used to play with Indian children near Minnehaha Creek.

"She used to go over and pester her dad and Victor and one day she climbed up a tree near where they were working and couldn't get down," said Polly. "This is what she told me happened:

She said, 'Victor, Victor, you have to help me down.'
'What will you give me if I get you down?' he asked her.
'I will marry you when I grow up,' she replied.
'Is that a promise?' he said."

After finishing the Lincoln house, Polly said, Victor Fridlund—who was a good ten years older than Mabel—headed for Willmar to practice his trade. He kept in touch with the Lincolns and when he returned to Minneapolis to live, he asked Mr. Lincoln if he could marry Mabel now. Mabel, who was then in her late teens, declined at first, Polly said, but Victor persisted. She liked Victor, Mabel said, but she didn't want to leave her mother. "He said, 'How about if I built a house next to your parents' house and we have a path between them so you can go see her whenever you want,'" Polly recounted. That did it and the two were married at the Lincoln home in 1904. Marilyn Brakke—their granddaughter and Polly's cousin—still has the white kid gloves both Victor and Mabel wore for their wedding and crumbled, dried rose petals that were in her wedding bouquet.

While they were waiting for Victor to finish the house on Dupont, they lived in a brand-new chicken coop close to the Creek. "Grandma always stressed that it was a new coop—no chickens had ever been in it," Polly said.

The Merchants Block—three separate buildings that included the White Star saloon—was torn down in 1961. This photo is taken at the intersection of Washington and Marquette Avenues in downtown Minneapolis. At this writing, the former Federal Reserve Bank occupied the space where the Merchants Block once stood. Photo by Bernie Vartdal, courtesy of Robert R. Johnson.

Axel Johnson
Keeper of the White Star

Washington Avenue in downtown Minneapolis has led an up-and-down existence and Axel Johnson—born Axel Ragnar Jonsson in Småland, Sweden—saw much of it happen. Johnson, who came to the United States in 1909, was trained as a tailor in Sweden, like his father and brothers and sister. "He didn't make the whole suit," said his son, Robert R. (Bob) Johnson. "In those days, each tailor specialized in one part of the suit. He was a pants maker." His family lived in a beautiful house, capped with gingerbread trim in the town of Nybro in Småland. "They were a prosperous family. My mother's family, on the other hand, were not as affluent. They lived in Västergötland and Småland in small villages farming the land."

His father and mother weren't very happy to see their son go to America, Bob said, but they finally gave him their permission. Unlike many other young men who wanted to go to the United States, he didn't need to get permission from the King as he was not old enough for military service. In fact, according to Bob, the most important reason why his father decided to leave Sweden was to avoid the nation's compulsory military service. He also wanted to see the world. He was just 17 years old when he left with a friend. They sailed on December 10, 1909 from Göteborg to Hull, England, across the North Sea. In typical immigrant fashion, they traveled by train from Hull to Southhampton. There they boarded the *S.S. Teutonic,* which was operated by the White Star Line. Axel Johnson turned 18 during the voyage. They landed on December 23rd in New York City and took the immigration train to Chicago.

When they got to Chicago, they had a layover of a few hours while they waited for the next train. Bob wrote about that day in a 1952 memoir about his dad: "About noon that day they were getting a little hungry. A fellow who could talk Swedish, for neither one of the boys could speak or understand a word of English, told them if they wanted to eat they should go across the street from the railroad station to a saloon. They had been told by train officials to stay in the station and not to go out and get lost in Chicago, but they went to the saloon to eat anyway. At that time you could buy a five-cent stein of beer and get a free lunch—all you could eat. My father thought this was great because he had never seen anything like it in the old country."

Axel soon got a job working as a tailor; he made ten dollars a week for working ten hours a day, six days a week. He bounced around a bit before settling down. He and his friend worked in Seattle, Washington, for a while and he worked briefly as a groundskeeper in Hillside Cemetery in Minneapolis. The cemetery job came with housing—on the edge of the cemetery. He stayed there even after quitting the job and returning to his tailor trade. Bob tells that his dad lived in the cemetery house during the winter, when no graves could be dug because the ground was frozen, and the coffins—with the dead inside—were kept stacked in a building to await burial after the ground thawed.

Although he had promised his mother and father to return to Sweden five years after he left, it was 1923 before he went back for a visit. He and Bob's mother—Edith Hildeen, who was raised in Mankato of Swedish-born parents—were married in 1926.

Axel Johnson worked as a tailor for some years before he made a big change in occupations and bought

Things had changed by this Christmas Eve in 1941 at the White Star saloon. More working men now patronized the bar. Axel Johnson is at the right behind the bar. Photo courtesy of Robert R. Johnson.

In the 1920s, the White Star saloon on Washington Avenue still had booths in the back, spittoons on the floor and open cigar boxes on one end of the bar. Axel Johnson is at the right behind the bar. Photo courtesy of Robert R. Johnson.

the White Star Lunch on Washington Avenue at its intersection with Marquette Avenue in 1929. It had been known as the White Star Saloon before Prohibition. "Dad bought it just before the crash," his son said. "I don't know what possessed him." Axel Johnson had never worked in a restaurant before buying it. The White Star had a long history. It was started as the Anderson and Sandberg Saloon in 1896, according to Bob, by a duo named—guess what—Ludwig Anderson and Andrew S. Sandberg.

The saloon was an elegant place, as photos show. It had a magnificent mahogany bar that Bob estimates was about 40 feet long. Part of the bar had hops—the grain used in making beer—carved into the front. Two sections of that bar are now in Bob's garage, waiting for him to restore them to their former beauty. A beautiful, eight-foot mahogany wall clock that hung on the wall of the saloon has already been restored and it is on the stairway landing wall in Bob's house in south Minneapolis. He also has a leaded, beveled glass mirror from the saloon in his dining room.

The White Star was a "dry" saloon when Axel Johnson bought it, as Prohibition had been in force since Jan. 16, 1920 nationally, although it began in Minneapolis on June 30, 1919, according to Bob. A lunch counter kept the place going and when Prohibition ended, business boomed. Beer was allowed to be sold in 1933 and hard liquor in 1934. "It was tough going during the Depression, but he managed to keep the business," Bob wrote in his memoir. Saloons then sold cigars and candy as well as liquid refreshments.

The White Star had a check cashing service with a teller cage. Axel Johnson worked long hours, six days a week, and sometimes went down on Sundays to check things over while the saloon was closed. Once in a while Bob would go along with him and sometimes Bob and his mother and sister would take the streetcar and eat their supper in the lunch area. Axel employed several bartenders. One, Charlie Holmgren, who came from Sweden in 1907, worked in the saloon for forty-two years, before and after Axel owned it.

The saloon was patronized by men only; photographs of the bar show not a woman in sight. Nearly all the men kept their hats on in those days. "At suppertime, five or six o'clock, that was the busy time," said Bob. "Men would come in after work and have a couple of drinks before they went home." Tap beer was the big seller, with the beer tapped from big barrels in the basement. "He was always trying to figure out how to get more glasses out of a barrel," said Bob.

Historically, the saloon business was somewhat seasonal, Bob says, as lumberjacks would come down to the cities from the woods in spring and summer and those who followed the harvest were in town more during the winter. Many men cashed their paychecks at the White Star. Axel charged them a nickel for that service. Spittoons were spaced evenly on the floor by the bar. "It was a classy saloon originally, but after Prohibition ended it became a working class bar." Nearly all of the patrons were Scandinavians, as most ethnic groups at that time had their "own" saloons. On Saturday nights, Axel would generally have someone playing an accordion or fiddle for tips. Some of the Swedish customers were reminded of home by the large oil painting of Kalmar Castle in Småland that hung on one wall.

Axel's wife kept the books for the saloon and she laid down the law to her husband. "She told him, 'You can't do both. If you're behind the bar, you can't drink.'" As

he grew up, Bob was a little embarrassed to say his dad ran a saloon. It was a job that carried a bit of a social stigma and it set him apart. Also, his dad worked long hours and often ate his supper at the saloon and didn't get home until late. "Other guys' fathers would be home at night and on Saturdays," said Bob.

Axel's occupation was also frowned upon by the church he wanted to join. Bob's mother put all the family's names down to be charter members of a Lutheran church forming in south Minneapolis. But Axel was turned down because he owned a bar. Bob and his mother and sister did join, however. His dad apparently took the slight well, said Bob. "Dad never said anything. They wouldn't let him be a member but they never turned his money down. I think he was more of a Christian than a lot of Christians. He would help people out, families that he came into contact with at the White Star that needed help."

As time passed, Axel bought the building the saloon was in, which had a 42-room hotel on the two stories above. The rooms were cheap. The other two buildings in the Merchants Block—regarded as a single building but actually three separate entities—also had hotels above the businesses below. Originally built in 1882 as offices for businessmen, the hotels had cheap rooms, but weren't the so-called flop houses, Bob said. "There were rooms across the street and in other old buildings where the owner had divided the rooms into smaller cubicles with chicken wire overhead; they were called cages or chicken coops."

In later years, Washington Avenue went steadily downhill. Axel sold the business in 1948, before it bottomed out. He was only 56 when he sold it, and took his family to Sweden for a visit that included a fancy family wedding. Axel always liked to look nice, his son said. "He always had tailor-made clothes and drove a Cadillac. He didn't drive until he was 44 years old and then he went in and bought a car and the salesman had to teach him how to drive so he could get home with the car."

Axel Johnson didn't stress his Swedish heritage much to his son, but Bob has delved into it on his own. He studied Swedish and has encouraged his four children to value their heritage. His interest in antique cars has led him to do research on the cars owned by Swan J. Turnblad, a Swedish immigrant who owned the first commercially manufactured automobile in Minneapolis, which he bought in 1900. Turnblad also built the house that is now the American Swedish Institute. Bob and his wife, June, are members of the Institute and so are their kids. Bob remembers going there in the 1940s with his parents, who were early members of the Institute.

The White Star and the other businesses in the Merchants Block were torn down in 1961 as part of the massive redevelopment project of what had become a skid row. Ironically, four decades later, the area is bouncing back and trendy bars and restaurants are once more popping up. It took a long time, but Washington Avenue is finally coming full circle.

Axel Johnson and his family returned to Sweden for a family wedding in 1948. They dressed formally for the occasion. It is the only time, according to Bob Johnson, that he ever wore tails. Bob Johnson is at right in the photo. His parents are to the left and his sister is next to Bob. Photo courtesy of Robert R. Johnson.

Chapter Five

Swedes at Play

Saturday Night Fever—Swedish Style

Yes, the Swedes were hard workers, but they played hard, too. The dance halls were legendary and many a match was made on the dance floor. Music was always a part of Swedish and Swedish-American celebrations and it still is. The St. Paul Swedish Men's Chorus is more than 100 years old and the newest entrant in the Scandinavian music scene—the annual Nordic Roots Festival—is drawing renewed attention to Scandinavian music. Professionals like Cliff Brunzell and his dad before him have entertained several generations of Twin City Swedes. One person who remembers waltzing at the South Side Auditorium where the elder Brunzell managed the dance hall is Gunhild Anderson. The Brunzell and Anderson stories are told in this chapter. Accompanying Cliff Brunzell's story is a peek at the minutes of the meetings of the long-gone Corona Band, in which his uncle played. Here also is the touching tale of folk dancer John P. Wallberg and his daughter and pal, Lorraine Wallberg McGrath.

Cliff Brunzell
The Man with the Golden Strings

When Cliff Brunzell was a boy in the late twenties and early thirties, Cedar Avenue was the meeting place for Swedish immigrants and their families. Many immigrants, including Cliff's parents, lived in the area and they flocked to Cedar Avenue, otherwise known as "Snoose Boulevard," on Saturday nights. And—always—where there were Swedes, there was music. "That's where the dance bands flourished," said the dapper Cliff. "There were probably forty of them in Minneapolis and many of them were on or close to Cedar. Social life did center around the dance halls. There weren't telephones in every home and few radios, mostly just crystal sets."

The dance halls always had live music and one of the best-known dance bands was the Oscar Danielson Orchestra. Cliff's dad, Herbert Brunzell, played the piano in the Orchestra. Playing violin was Ted Johnson, a well-known local musician. Danielson, the band leader, was the drummer and singer. "They called him the sausage maker from Sweden," Cliff said, with a chuckle. The band members, who made records for Columbia and RCA Victor, specialized in waltzes, polkas, schottisches and other dance tunes. None of the musicians had had much training. "When you're talented, you can make a lot of music without a lot of lessons," Cliff said.

Cliff Brunzell gives a lively performance of old-time Swedish dance tunes as he and his band—a reconstruction of the Oscar Danielson Orchestra—perform at the American Swedish Institute in Minneapolis. Photo courtesy of Cliff Brunzell.

The South Side Auditorium sometimes held masquerade dances, such as this one held on Thanksgiving evening in about 1911. Herbert Brunzell, co-manager of the dance hall is probably at right in the front row, next to the man carrying the large box. His partner, Hans Strom, wearing a dark suit and tie, stands next to the man in the police uniform in the front row. In the background, signs in English and Swedish announce dance nights. Photo courtesy of Cliff Brunzell.

When radio came in, the band performed on "Call of the North," a weekly program on WCCO-radio.

Herbert Brunzell also was co-manager, from 1921 to 1931, of the South Side Auditorium, one of the most popular dance halls. The auditorium was on the third floor of a building at Third Street and Twelfth Avenue, just a few blocks from Cedar. The building is long gone, but Cliff remembers it well. "The dance hall was vast, in my mind," he said. Brunzell and his family spent a lot of time at the South Side and the results of being around music were not surprising. "It had a great impact on me. It made you want to do something like that. I had to be in that, too."

His parents, Elma Larson Brunzell and Herbert Brunzell, knew each other in Sweden before they came to the United States around 1910. They settled in Minneapolis and Cliff was born in 1921 in the family home near Minnehaha Falls. Later, the family moved

Cliff Brunzell, center, has been the leader of the Golden Strings since the group organized. Photo courtesy of Cliff Brunzell.

near the Mississippi River, on Seabury Avenue, and Cliff went to Seward Elementary School through the eighth grade and then to South High School, where he played violin in the concert orchestra and also was a member of a jazz trio that performed for pep fests. "That was quite unique to have a jazz trio play for pep fests," he said. His interest in jazz violin is still great and in 1991 he was pleased to receive the jazz violinist award at the Minnesota Music Awards Festival. He recently released a CD featuring his jazz trio of violin, guitar and bass.

Cliff has been playing the violin for most of his 80 years. "There was a three-quarter size violin in the house and my brother was supposed to be learning it. I picked it up and created a tune. I was eight and a half years old." Lessons quickly followed. "I had a paper route to pay for violin lessons at first. They cost a dollar. Then I went to study at MacPhail and that cost three dollars a lesson, but the teacher, J. Rudolph Peterson, reduced it to two dollars because he knew we couldn't afford it."

Whenever he played in public, his family always came to support him. "My parents, my brother and sister, my relatives were wonderful. They were a rooting section for me." His large, extended family had many gatherings and there was always music at them, with a lot of singing. "I miss them very much, " he said sadly.

"God bless my parents for giving me a chance in life. Talent is fine, a good teacher is fine, but the rest is work. It's still work. If you are conscientious, and I am, you go about it very seriously." Cliff, who still plays more than 200 engagements a year, still practices. "I have the foundation, but I practice to maintain it. You've really got to sweat—it's the price of learning.

As for performing, Cliff said, "You've got to maintain the edge. You can't say to yourself, 'I've played this a hundred times.' Keeping the edge when you play something familiar is a wonderful attitude and all good performers have it. If I played the program five years ago and I'm still doing it exactly the same way, there's something wrong. If you travel, you can get away with that, but when you play locally, you can't." Even the occasional thin crowd doesn't bother him. "I think to myself, 'Remember, you might be playing for some people for the first time.'"

The late Al Sheehan, who was his friend and agent, once gave him advice that he still follows. "After I was complaining about being on edge because I had to repeat a show I had just played ten minutes ago, Al said to me, 'Cliff, don't ever lose it. You're like a race horse; get up for the show.'"

Cliff is perhaps best known locally for his years as the founder and leader of "The Golden Strings," which played in the Flame Room at Curt Carlson's Radisson Hotel in downtown Minneapolis. He almost missed this legendary gig. "I didn't even want the job. I was having good luck playing freelance jobs." But he took it, hired other string players and the music began. "We've played 15,000 shows from memory, with three shows a night five or six nights a week in the earlier years."

Why, long past the age when most people retire, does he keep playing for audiences? "I'm good at it, I like it and I like meeting people," said the genial Cliff, whose youthful appearance and demeanor belie his age. "Your talent is God's gift to you. What you give to others is a gift to God."

He was already a very good violinist when he enlisted during World War II. He had hopes that he would be able to use his musical ability in the service and he said, with only a slight exaggeration, "I'd say, 'I'm Cliff "Violin"

Brunzell and I live in "Violin" Minnesota.' I tried to emphasize that I was an accomplished violinist." The Army being the Army, he found himself assigned to the tank corps at Fort Knox, Kentucky. "I brought my violin with me and I played in the barracks and on local base radio shows. Finally, I decided I'd like to die a little cleaner than in the tank service. We'd go on bivouac, in the rain and the mud and the dust. I didn't like it." Eventually, he was transferred to flight school and became a B-25 bomber pilot for the Army Air Force.

When the war ended, he went back to Minnesota and wound up at MacPhail again. All of his education was paid for by the GI Bill. "I don't know where I would have been without it," he said. Cliff piled up an impressive three degrees—a bachelor's degree in music with a violin major and a second bachelor of music degree with a major in music education, plus a master's degree in violin, all from the MacPhail School of Music.

"My parents were educated only through the eighth grade, but they always believed in education. "They can't take an education away from you," said Cliff, who believes that education can come from many sources. "There were five major educational influences in my life. Number one was the military, two was playing in a major world symphony, the Minneapolis Symphony Orchestra, three was a formal education, four was being a public school music teacher and five is having lived a long time—life is a great teacher."

He traveled widely with the Symphony, which is now the Minnesota Orchestra. Under conductor Antal Dorati, the Symphony went on several major tours. "We played in Baghdad, Tehran, Athens, Thessalonica, Belgrade, Zagreb, Karachi, Istanbul, Ankara, Bombay and Lahore," he reeled off the names quickly. He later taught music in Hopkins schools and encouraged young people to be musicians. He founded and directed the Metropolitan Youth Orchestra from 1960–64.

Cliff met his wife, Jean, a professional pianist and teacher, while both were studying at MacPhail. They have been married for more than fifty years. She teaches piano students at the Brunzell's home in south Minneapolis. Their two daughters are musical, also. "We have a lot of music when we get together. For our 50th anniversary, we had an eight-piece orchestra here and most of the players were family members."

His has been a life full of fun, experiences and, above all, music. And now, harking back to the dance halls of his childhood, Cliff has returned to the music he first knew. He has recreated the Oscar Danielson Orchestra and he and his band mates perform the beloved old dance tunes in occasional performances at the American Swedish Institute in Minneapolis, talking about the old days and old music between tunes. At the end, he salutes his heritage by playing what must be the unofficial Swedish-American anthem, *Hälsa dem därhemma* on his still-golden strings.

"Hälsa" may be his theme song when he plays old-time music, but he also considers it entrepreneur Curt Carlson's song. Carlson, who owned the Radisson Hotel where Cliff played for so many years, loved the song and Brunzell tried to play it sometime during a show when Carlson was in the audience. When Carlson died, his family asked Cliff to play it at his funeral. Now, Cliff said, whenever he spots the Carlson family in an audience while he is playing, he plays "their" song to them.

Hälsa dem därhemma

Published in 1922 by Wilhelm Hansen in Copenhagen, Denmark. Words (in Swedish) by C. H. Bengtsson; music by Elith Worsing.

Hälsa dem därhemma,
Hälsa far och mor,
Hälsa gröna hagen,
Hälsa lille bror.
Om jag hade vingar,
Flöge jag med dig,
Svala flyg mot hemmet,
Hälsa ifrån mig

The English translation below is a literal one, by Anne Gillespie Lewis.

Greet those at home,
Greet father and mother,
Greet green fields,
Greet little brother.
If I had wings,
I would fly with you.
Swallow flying homeward,
Greet them from me.

There was a reason why Cedar Avenue in Minneapolis got the nickname "Snoose Boulevard"—and the reason was a little round cardboard box with a silver top and "Copenhagen" printed on it. The Copenhagen boxes were tightly packed with snuff, or *Snus* in Swedish and Norwegian, which was more often spelled phonetically as "Snoose." Cedar Avenue was a haven for Scandinavian immigrants—many of them snuff users—in the decades of the late nineteenth and early twentieth century and somewhere along the line the name "Snoose Boulevard" came into use and it stuck. There were other so-called "Snoose Boulevards," including Payne Avenue in St. Paul, but Cedar is the street most closely associated with the nickname.

Snuff users usually carried the boxes in the breast pocket of their shirt, jacket or overalls. You could often tell snuff users from the round impression the snuff box left on their clothes. "Many people used snuff and it was a dirty, nasty habit. You put it between your gum and your lip. The snuff made the men spit all the time. My dad used it," said Cliff Brunzell. With all the spitting going on, did walkers have to watch their step so they didn't slip and slid down Cedar? "Ooooh, yes," said Cliff emphatically. He never used snuff himself, but he loves to slip into the character of an old Swede on Cedar and say this tongue-twister to audiences during his performances of old-time Scandinavian songs. Say it out loud, but please don't spit when you're done: "Ole, yew yewstew yews snus, yewsent yew?"

Oscar Danielson was a member of the Corona Band. Later, he played in the Oscar Danielson Orchestra. Members of the Orchestra, from left, are Nels Dalin, guitar; Oscar Danielson, drums and vocal; Carl Danielson, tuba; Bert Danielson, accordian; Herbert Brunzell, piano; and Ted Johnson, violin. The photo was taken around 1931 at the South Side Auditorium. Photo courtesy of Cliff Brunzell.

The life and times of the Corona Band

There were many so-called Swedish bands in the Twin Cities in the early part of the twentieth century. Live music was played at the numerous dance halls that drew Swedish immigrants on weekends. Most of the bands formed, flourished for a while, and then vanished, leaving little trace. Luckily, the story of one concert band survives in an old black ledger, bound with maroon on the spine and the corners. Cliff Brunzell, who leads his own band and can recall the Swedish bands, has the ledger now. It is mostly in Swedish, with a bit of English thrown in. The English translation is by Anne Gillespie Lewis. It begins in 1921 and ends in 1926, with no indication that the group had disbanded, although there were signs that all was not well. All quotes and information below are taken from the ledger.

The account begins:

"The following short report is a history of a Swedish band in Minneapolis . . . its origin or beginning.

"At Svithiod Lodge's general meeting at Tonka Bay [west of the Twin Cities, on Lake Minnetonka, ed.] in July of 1921, some members of the former Norden Band met together there with the leader of the Harmonia Choir and the undersigned [Conrad Mattson], who talked about . . . the need for a Swedish band in the city of Minneapolis."

The group decided to meet again at Mattson's house in North Minneapolis in August and, meanwhile, to try to interest other Swedish musicians in the effort. Twelve men showed up and they decided to meet regularly at the New Viking Hall every Sunday "with whatever instruments we can obtain."

The band got a loan of $200 from a lodge, chose a committee to obtain instruments, chose officers and decided on the name "Corona Band," all within a few weeks. No reason is given for choosing the name. Members were charged $5 to join the band. Original members, and the instruments they played, were: Oscar Olson, band leader; Gust Newquist, cornet; Conrad Mattson, clarinet; Herman Sundberg, alt. [alto horn]; Carl Danielson, alt; Oscar Larson, bass; Holger Larson, cornet and saxophone; Oscar Danielson, drums; Alfrid Frolund, baritone; Fred Brunzell [Cliff Brunzell's uncle], bass; Selfrid Johnson, cornet; C. H. Nordby, clarinet; Sam Johnson, clarinet; and Victor E. Nordlöf, alt. Several were later to become members of the legendary Oscar Danielson Orchestra.

Their first public performance was for their benefactor, the Blenda Lodge. The band played for the Lodge on Oct. 25, 1921, and received ten dollars. On November 8, they played for free for Mrs. Klara Larson's birthday party at the Yeoman Hall. They cleared $79.50 at a dance they organized on Dec. 14 and worked steadily around town for organizations, private parties and dances. The take varied greatly: they took a loss for one dance and made $65 in June of 1922 playing for the Norden Lodge. Income for 1921 was $469, including the $200 from the loan. Expenses totaled $272.38, including $5.50 for a B-flat baritone horn, $50 for a bass tuba, $10 for an honorarium for the leader, Oscar Olson, small sums for repairing instruments, rent and tickets and a minuscule amount for interest on the loan. The band cleared $196.62 for the year. Gigs kept coming in, and monthly income climbed, even though the band continued to play gratis on some occasions. The loan from the lodge was paid in full in March of 1922.

Meetings were conducted according to the proper protocol, with motions made, discussed, and frequently tabled, and numerous committees named for every new venture. Sometimes nearly all the band members were named to committees.

Band members came and went, some under most unharmonious circumstances. After one man resigned, it was pointed out that he "didn't follow our regulations and didn't work for the band's best, partly by causing doubt within the band and partly through missing rehearsals or performances with poor or no excuses altogether," according to the minutes of the September, 1922, meeting. The lament continued: "The band had gone to great expense to buy a clarinet especially for his use [and] we can't get the original price back." After more discussion about the man and deciding not to let him have any proceeds of the band, the record states sternly: "This example [is] a warning to all members . . . each and every one, not any one in particular, to follow our regulations and take an interest in our band's welfare. If the band will have a future, there must be discipline within our organization and punctuality and interest is required from each and every member."

At one point, band members dreamed of bigger things. The July, 1922, minutes reported: "A question came up about the possibility for the band making a trip to Sweden in the summer of 1923, the question was of unusual interest and all members were in agreement about possibly making the trip. A committee was formed . . . to make inquiries of various steamship companies about the possibility of cheap passage." No other mention is made about that plan to tour Sweden, although there was later some correspondence about another Swedish trip, which fizzled. Cliff Brunzell said

he never knew of his uncle, or any other band members, making a Swedish tour.

The band had fun, too. The meticulous records for expenses show sums for ice cream and rehearsal treats, and—once—$1.50 for beer. Outings were frequent. The whole band was invited to Herman Sundberg's cottage for a picnic in May of 1922. At the February, 1923, business meeting they planned a big picnic at Parker's Lake for the first of July and talked about holding a drawing for a Ford touring car to build up the band's funds. Unlike some of their ideas, the raffle for the Ford was a big success. The band made a down payment of $25, then sold nearly $500 worth of tickets for the car. The Ford cost them $331 altogether, for a handsome profit of nearly $170.

The February meeting also brought about a big change in the band: the editor of *Svenska Amerikanska Posten*, the leading Swedish language newspaper in Minnesota, came before the group and offered to become their business manager if they were willing to change the band's name to "Posten Band." The editor, Mr. Martinson, promised to do everything possible to boost the band "by advertising and making us known in Swedish circles through his newspaper." The band members were thrilled and changed the name on the spot.

Although there is no mention of discord until much later and the band's take continued to rise, some of the members may have been unhappy with their new arrangement with *Posten*. Minutes for the meeting of the 10th of March 1924, note tersely that Oscar Danielson, the drummer who was later to form a well-known band that carried his name, resigned. An emergency meeting followed on March 19th. Band leader Fred Brunzell opened the three-hour meeting, as the minutes recorded, "with the discouraging question of whether there were any ideas about reorganizing the band or whether it should be disbanded altogether. But since there was no answer to the question, he went on to the next point."

The next point was the resignation of Martinson as business manager. Later, a band member asked whether Oscar Danielson, who had just resigned, could be allowed to speak. A 'huge' discussion ensued, finally petering out, with Danielson standing his ground. Later in the meeting, Danielson and another band member who had resigned earlier took back their resignations. The band limped along, with more resignations, a vote to resign from the union, a resolution to use English in both the minutes and at work, so as to encourage new members who weren't Swedish, and—after much dithering—a decision to drop the *Posten* name and take back their original name. Apparently they didn't learn from past entanglements, however; in one of the last meetings recorded, they toyed with the idea of becoming the band for the newly constructed Eagles Lodge. The final entry is for the meeting of Aug. 3, 1926, with members still talking about switching to English and hiring halls for concerts and dances. And so it is nice to assume that the band played on.

Gunhild Karlsson Anderson
The girl who loved to dance

Gunhild Anderson is every Minnesotan's idea of a Swedish grandmother now. Tiny, with gray hair and a sweet smile, Gunhild speaks softly and patiently and loves to feed company her Swedish specialties. But the 91-year-old Gunhild was once a carefree girl who loved

Gunhild is shown wearing her Dalarna folk dress, while Maureen wears the traditional Medelpad folk dress. Photo courtesy of Gunhild Anderson.

to dance. Even now, it isn't hard to imagine her whirling on the dance floor to the tune of old Swedish favorite songs.

Sixteen-year-old Gunhild Linnea Karlsson and her sister Margit, who was a year older, sailed from Göteborg on May 17, 1926. They were bound for Minnesota, where their father had already arrived. Their mother was left behind in Avesta, Dalarna. "We weren't sad to leave Sweden; it was an adventure."

The girls were in good company: also on the brand new *Gripsholm* were Sweden's Crown Prince Gustaf Adolf and his bride, Princess Louise, who were on their honeymoon. The girls traveled third class and the most exciting thing was when the royal pair came down and had dinner with the third class passengers and danced among them later. Gunhild and the others were told not to approach the royal pair. Little did Gunhild know then that one day she would welcome King Carl XVI Gustaf of Sweden—grandson of the honeymooning couple—into her home in south Minneapolis.

The sisters whiled away the hours walking on deck and getting acquainted with the other passengers. "But between breakfast, lunch and dinner, we were so busy," Gunhild said with a laugh. It was quite an event when they saw "one of those large whales" on the trip.

After ten days, Gunhild and her sister arrived in the evening in New York City. Because the ship docked at night, they had to stay on board overnight. In the morning they debarked at Ellis Island and had a complete physical. Each immigrant at that time had to arrive with 25 dollars. Five of these dollars were taken and in return the girls got a bag of food. It contained bread, summer sausage, sardines, an apple and an orange. "That's all we had for the trip to Minneapolis," said Gunhild.

When they boarded the train for Minnesota, they were delighted to find a box of chocolates on their seat. "We said, 'Oh, how nice these Americans are,' and we opened the box up. Then a man came down the aisle, asking for a dollar for the candy, so we had to pay him because we'd opened it."

Their father met them at the train. He had a job working for a carpenter. Gunhild and Margit stayed with their uncle and auntie at first. They had a whirlwind tour of the city and remember going to Minnehaha Park, where they and their family had a photo taken by a statue of Gunnar Wennerberg. Years later, the two sisters returned to the park and the statue to have another picture taken.

"We got jobs right away," said Gunhild. Like many young Swedish immigrant women, she and her sister worked as hired girls or cooks for wealthy families.

When Gunhild and her sister, Margit, arrived in Minneapolis, they stayed with their aunt and uncle in North Minneapolis. Gunhild is at the back in this photo, with her father, Carl Carlson, at her side. Others in the photo are members of her aunt and uncle's family. Photo courtesy of Gunhild Anderson.

Gunhild's first job was with a Swedish-American family at 2800 Dean Boulevard, near Lake Calhoun. "She was very particular," said Gunhild. "She was always saying, 'Have you dusted in that corner? Have you dusted behind the door?'"

Gunhild and her sister, who worked at 34th Street and Garfield Avenue South, both had Thursday afternoon and evening off, as well as Sundays. On the other days, they worked from breakfast time until after supper. "Our dad came and got us on Thursday afternoons and showed us how to take the streetcar and how to transfer if we were going to our auntie's and uncle's house in north Minneapolis." They also spent their free time shopping downtown, often eating a meal out at the Hasty Tasty Café, where less than one dollar would buy a lunch.

The family she worked for moved to Lake Minnetonka during the summer. The lake, a sprawling expanse of water, with many bays and inlets, was a fashionable destination for Twin City residents who could afford to escape the heat and humidity of the cities. "I was more or less a lady's companion. We went fishing in the lake every day. I rowed the boat and she trolled for fish." Also on the lakeshore was a park and clubhouse owned by the Svithiod Society. During summer, dances were held there and Gunhild eagerly participated. "It was a lovely place and we loved to dance there." In the fall, the family returned to Minneapolis and Gunhild visited her auntie and uncle and met a lot of young Swedish immigrants her own age.

Gunhild didn't speak any English when she arrived, but it hardly mattered. "We only associated with Swedish people," she said. Nevertheless, she soon saw the need to learn English and she and her sister enrolled in evening classes at Washington School. They attended two or three winter terms, and were soon at home in English. "After a year, we could manage pretty well."

The evening lessons at the school had another benefit. "The school was old and had wooden floors. There was a girl in the office who could play piano and we could dance in the hall at intermission." Dancing was a big part of Gunhild's life from an early age and she continued dancing until her nineties—old Swedish dances such as the hambo, the schottische, the polka and also the waltz. The orchestras often played Scandinavian songs such as *Kom, lilla flicka, valsa med mej* ("Come, little girl, waltz with me") and one of Gunhild's favorite songs, *When it's Springtime in the Rockies*.

Her employer was protective of the light-hearted young girl and didn't always approve of her dancing and coming home late. "One night, I stayed until they closed the doors at the South Side Auditorium. The streetcars had quit running, so I had to walk from Hennepin and Lake to 2800 Dean Boulevard. The next morning, my employer said to me, 'Where were you last night?' After that, I went out to look for a different job." Gunhild speaks kindly of this woman, however, who helped her in many ways.

Her second job was with the Thomas K. Kelly family, who lived at 2316 Pillsbury Avenue, "I was supposed to be the cook and my sister was the second floor maid." Next she went to work for a Jewish family. Years later, she called on the grandson of her employer. She went to his office and asked to see him, telling his secretary only, "You can tell him it's a voice from the past." Intrigued, the man came out of his inner office and was moved to tears reminiscing with Gunhild about his grandmother. Gunhild earned $6 a week on her first job, $7 for her second and was up to $11 per week when she married. Room and board were provided by each household.

Throughout her different jobs and until recent years, Gunhild kept on dancing. "Margit and I went to Gustavus Adolphus Hall, on 17th Avenue and Lake Street almost always on Thursday evenings and we always went together. We met all our friends there. There were so many immigrants. It was like a family." "Prize dances" were often held during the evenings. "I was in those contests all the time," said Gunhild. She often won, too, though the only "prize" was usually just the honor of being chosen the winner.

The dance clubs have a special meaning for Gunhild. "On one of our first trips there, we were standing on the side, and Margit said to me, 'See that guy over there, he's going to come and ask you for a dance.'" She was right. Hilding Anderson, who had immigrated to the United States from the province of Medelpad, Sweden, asked the petite Gunhild to dance. He also—eventually—asked her to marry him. She was 17 when they met and 21 when they were married by the pastor of the First Swedish Baptist Church in 1930. By that time, her sister Margit had moved to Chicago, where she later married.

The Andersons were married in the pastor's home and had a reception at Franklin and Elliot Avenues. "The buildings are still there. It was two Swedish ladies who made the meal for us. They made meatballs and they were so hard you could hardly eat them! We were married on a Saturday and Hilding went to work on Monday morning." Hilding worked for Ohleen Dairy for about forty years, doing various jobs and winding up as a milkman. Gunhild worked as a sand technician for Minneapolis Moline for 27 years. The Andersons had one child, Maureen Linnea.

Gunhild wore a satin wedding dress that she bought for $19 at Leader's Department Store when she married Hilding Anderson on November 1, 1930—Halmrast Studios. Photo courtesy of Gunhild Anderson.

Hilding Anderson, like many other Swedish immigrants and their descendants, worked for a creamery. In his case, it was Ohleen Dairy Company in south Minneapolis. He worked inside bottling milk and making butter at first and later was a residential milkman. He is in the back row, third from left, in this photo taken about 1931. Photo courtesy of Gunhild Anderson.

They started off married life in a small apartment on 15th Avenue and 22nd Street, later moved to a one-bedroom apartment at 1911 11th Avenue South and finally moved to their house at 16th Avenue and 50th Street, where they lived for 40-some years. In later years, they moved from the house to the apartment where Gunhild currently lives.

Dancing remained part of Gunhild's life during her early married years. "When my baby was small, I'd just bundle her up and take her along to the dance." Gunhild's social life revolved around the dance halls, and she met many of her longtime friends there.

Gunhild had to learn to cook Swedish food after she married. Her mother, who had joined the rest of the family in Minnesota, preferred American to Swedish food, so Gunhild had to recreate many of the foods of her childhood by experimenting and by chatting with her friends "When I worked for American families, I cooked what they wanted. After I got married I got back to cooking Swedish food." The foods that she recalled and still makes were the dishes poor people could afford—rutabagas and potatoes cooked together, yellow pea soup, meatballs. "We were poor in Sweden," said Anderson. "Sometimes we had a cow, sometimes we had a goat. We ate very little meat and rutabagas were one of the few things we could have year-round."

Now Gunhild always has her special rye bread baked and Swedish meatballs made and tucked in the freezer in case company drops by. Like most grandmothers, Gunhild likes to see her visitors eat. Annette Bittner, who works at the American Swedish Institute in Minneapolis where Gunhild is a volunteer in the bookstore on Wednesday afternoons, often visits her on Thursday evenings to speak Swedish and have a Swedish supper.

"She goes all out," said Bittner. "The table is set in the most perfect Swedish style and she'll make dishes you'd think you could only get in Sweden. And she keeps saying, *'ät nu, ät nu!'* (Eat now, eat now!)"

She is still making Swedish favorites for friends, family and—yes—even for the King of Sweden and his Queen. The royal couple came to call on Gunhild and Hilding, in order to meet a typical Swedish immigrant

Gunhild loved to bake and cook, so it's no wonder she posed jauntily, sometime in the 1940s, with what appears to be a brand new stove. Photo courtesy of Gunhild Anderson.

couple, during a trip to Minnesota in 1981. Gunhild served them her homebaked cardamom bread and cookies made by volunteers at the American Swedish Institute.

The visit was preceded by weeks of planning. When Gunhild first got a call from John Lofgren, who was at that time director at the American Swedish Institute, her first reaction was, *"Är du tokig?"* (Are you crazy?). Assured that the King and Queen did indeed want to visit the Andersons, Gunhild plunged into a flurry of housecleaning. The hardest part, she said, was to keep the visit secret until it was officially announced.

When the day finally arrived, the royal pair visited with the Andersons as if the four were old friends. They toured the house, had a drink and ate the goodies Gunhild set before them. When it came time for them to go, Gunhild impulsively hugged the King and said, "Oh, I wish you could stay overnight with us." The King hugged her back and said, "I wish we could, too." Unfortunately, the next time Gunhild saw the King and Queen, Hilding Anderson had died. The Queen, who remembered the visit well, told Gunhild how sorry she was.

Hilding, Gunhild said, always wanted to return to Sweden to live after he retired. Though she loved to return to Sweden—the couple went back for visits eight times, the last in 1982—Gunhild resisted his suggestion of living there. "All he ever got to thinking about was going to Sweden," said Gunhild. "He wanted to go back to live and he couldn't understand why I didn't want to. I am Swedish; you won't take that away from me, but I feel more American. I became a citizen in 1929 and then I could vote and I've never given up that privilege." Gunhild's daughter, Maureen, who had married and had two children, took Gunhild's part. "Who's going to put flowers on your grave if you go to Sweden?" she asked her mother.

The couple had still not decided finally what to do when Hilding got sick. They had booked another trip to Sweden and already had the tickets when he died. Sadly, their daughter Maureen also died of cancer a couple of years later. Gunhild misses them greatly, but keeps busy with her friends and her volunteer work at the American Swedish Institute, where she is greatly loved and cherished. And when she smiles and laughs, you can see the young girl dancing in her merry eyes.

Gunhild was well-known for her knack with breads and cookies. For years, she was one of the mainstays in baking for the American Swedish Institute's annual Christmas bazaar. After the bazaar came Lucia Day, on December 13. Many people still use her recipe for *lussekatter*, the saffron-flavored buns served on that day. The recipe for Swedish Rye Bread—which the Swedes call *limpa*—below, is a cooperative effort of Gunhild and two friends, Helga Sparrman and Ingrid Brunzell, who were the same age and were also Swedish immigrants. "We met at different dance halls and we would compare each other's recipes," said Anderson.

"It isn't fair for me to have all the credit," Anderson gently insisted. "The three of us shared ideas. For instance, if we made head cheese, we'd compare the spices we used. None of us had telephones when we first met, so we'd often meet on Saturday night at Swedish dance clubs."

The women kept up their friendship as their children were born and grew up. "Ingrid Brunzell passed away last year, but I still talk to Helga every week," said Anderson.

Jenny Johnson, left, Gunhild and Daisy Samuelson spent hours baking goodies for events at the American Swedish Institute. Here they are in the 1980s preparing for the annual Christmas bake sale. Photo courtesy of Gunhild Anderson.

The rye bread Gunhild makes is a very light rye that calls for medium rye flour, which is available at most supermarkets. Be patient when making *limpa*. The overnight process gives the yeast a chance to ferment. Remember, the longer you knead the bread, the finer the texture will be. Slice the bread thinly for the best results. The recipe can be doubled exactly for six loaves, but if you double the recipe, you may need to use a mixer to incorporate most of the flour and work in the rest by hand.

Postscript: Gunhild died on July 3, 2001. She worked in the bookstore in the American Swedish Institute until six months before her death. She was the heart and soul of the last great wave of Swedish immigration and she will be greatly missed.

Gunhild's Swedish Rye Bread (limpa)

1½ c. medium rye flour
2 c. milk (or use 1 c. milk and 1 c. water or 2 c. water
    in which potatoes have been boiled)
1 tbsp. yeast
½ tbsp. salt
½ c. melted butter or margarine
½ c. sugar
¼ c. dark Karo syrup
1 tbsp. caraway seed
1 tbsp. anise seed
approximately 6 c. unbleached white flour

The night before you want to bake the bread, combine rye flour, milk, yeast and salt in a large bowl, cover and let sit overnight. This does not have to be refrigerated. The next day, add the other ingredients, working in as much of the flour as possible, to make a stiff dough. Knead until the seeds start to fall out of the dough (approximately 5–8 minutes). Put dough back in the bowl and let rise until doubled in size. Punch down, turn out on a board and shape into three long loaves. Place on lightly greased large cookie sheet and let rise again until nearly doubled. Bake in an oven preheated to 400 degrees, but turn the temperature down to 350 when you put the loaves in. Bake until crust is golden brown (40–55 minutes). Brush immediately with melted butter. Makes three loaves.

Kom, lilla flicka, valsa med mej
Kom lilla flicka, valsa med mej, valsa med mej,
    valsa med mej!
Mitt under dansen kysser jag dej, fal-la-la-la-la lej.
Tra-la-la-la, tra-la-la-la, tra-la-la-la, tra-la-la-la!
Mitt under dansen kysser jag dej, fal-la-la-la-la lej.

(translation—Anne Gillespie Lewis)

"Come, little girl, waltz with me"
Come, little girl, waltz with me, waltz with me, waltz
    with me!
In the middle of the dance I'll kiss you,
    fa-la-la-la-la, lej.
Tra-la-la-la, tra-la-la-la, tra-la-la-la, tra-la-la-la!
In the middle of the dance I'll kiss you,
    fa-la-la-la-la, lej.

Jim McGrath, left, and Lorraine McGrath, are in Leksand, Dalarna, folk dress in this photo taken at Svenskarnas Dag at Minnehaha Park in the 1970s. Photo courtesy of Lorraine McGrath.

Lorraine Wallberg McGrath
Spinn, spinn, spinn, dottern min

Lorraine Wallberg McGrath lost her pal—her dad, John P. Wallberg—when she was just twelve years old. Sixty-five years have passed and she still gets teary eyed when she talks about him. And I understand, for my own pal—my father—died nearly fifty years ago when I was a child. And so, on a beautiful June afternoon at her home on the east side of St. Paul, we cried together and talked some more, and then we had a couple of cups of coffee and I gathered all my will power and managed to turn down Lorraine's offer of dessert. Anyone who knows what a good cook she is will know that was a heroic feat on my part. However, this is not my story, it is Lorraine's, so here it is.

Lorraine's dad, John Per Wallberg (he was Per Johan in Sweden) emigrated from Gävle, Sweden, on the Gulf of Bothnia, in 1912. He was scheduled to come over on the *Titanic,* but luckily for him it was overbooked. Lorraine never knew about the close call until she visited her relatives in Sweden many years after her father's death. "My parents talked a lot about the *Titanic,* but he never mentioned that he was supposed to be on it," said Lorraine.

John Wallberg left behind his parents, a sister and other relatives and many friends, whom he often mentioned in letters back home. Later in the year he left, his brother, Sven, was born. They never did meet each other and Sven died before Lorraine could meet him, either. John was an avid athlete at home and founded *Brynäs Idrottsförening,* a sport club near Gävle. Years later, Lorraine and her daughter, Kathy, were made honorary members of the club on a trip to Sweden.

John Wallberg was quite a joiner in Sweden and remained one when he settled in the United States. Over the years he belonged to several lodges, a dance group and a Swedish male chorus and performed on the same program as the beloved Swedish-American comedian who called himself *Olle i Skratthult.*

John Wallberg was a musician as well and brought his accordion with him when he came and soon played for special occasions. In the early years, he was playing the accordion and was overheard by Hilma Lindbloom, who traveled with the *Olle i Skratthult* act. Lindbloom told her friend Linnea Osman about the young man playing Swedish tunes on his accordion and Osman asked him to join her fledgling Swedish dance group.

The dancers, who later called themselves the Twin City Swedish Folk Dancers, were in great demand at

John Wallberg is at left in this photo, which was probably taken in the Twin Cities. The two other men are unidentified, but the accordion was Wallberg's. Photo courtesy of Lorraine McGrath.

Swedish celebrations, such as the Midsummer Day parties, which were first held in Phalen Park in St. Paul in the 1920s. They were the forerunner of the *Svenskarnas Dag* celebration, held since the 1930s at Minnehaha Park in Minneapolis. Osman, who married very late in life and had no children, became very good friends with the Wallbergs, and was so close that Lorraine speaks of her as though she were a member of the family. "She drove my mother and me home from the hospital when I was born and I was there on the night Linnea died," said Lorraine. "We were at Linnea's apartment on holidays. In summertime we had picnics and did a lot of swimming. I used to follow her around so much that her sister said I was safety pinned to Linnea's skirt."

John Wallberg was married and had a young son when he started dancing with Linnea's group. Lorraine was born in 1924, when her brother was 10 years old and she was the apple of her father's eye. He saw that she joined the junior dance group that Linnea started and she danced with the junior group from the time she was three years old until she "graduated" to the senior group at the age of 16. "Once the junior group went to Chicago to dance and I think there were 45 kids in one hotel room, sleeping every which way. One was even sleeping in the bathtub. I don't know how Linnea did it. She had a real way about her," said Lorraine.

As important as Linnea was to Lorraine, her dad was an even stronger force. "My father taught me to dance. He taught me, *Spinn, spinn, spinn, dottern min* [Spin, Spin, Spin, Daughter Mine] and other songs. He made a real Swede out of me. He taught us a lot about Sweden."

Linnea Osman, who led the Twin City Folkdancers for many years, wore an elaborate headdress when she was Midsummer Queen at Lake Phalen in the 1920s. Lorraine McGrath said thousands of people attended the celebration, which was the forerunner of Svenskarnas Dag. *Photo courtesy of Lorraine McGrath.*

John Wallberg had to quit dancing when he was still young. He had contracted rheumatic fever as a young man after coming to North America. The fever weakened his heart and he became weaker over the years.

While he had to stop dancing, he continued to sing as a member of the St. Paul Swedish Male Chorus. In addition to his illness, times were tough financially. He and a friend, Fredolf Alfaby, owned a fur processing company in Robbinsdale, a Minneapolis suburb, but the firm went under during the Depression. Then he tried selling vacuum cleaners. "He sold Hoovers door to door. For a man as proud as he was, it was difficult for him," said Lorraine.

Her dad's poor health meant that the family had to rely on her brother's income. "My father couldn't do much. He would get so tired. My brother had to quit school and work as a butcher to support us. Harold would come home at noon for *middag* [noon meal]. We always had Swedish food to eat. We all loved to laugh at our house. When the four of us would sit around the table we'd get the giggles. My mother would have this little laugh, like 'heh, heh, heh' and my father would laugh without making a sound, just his shoulders shaking, and my brother and I would laugh really loud. In fact, I went into the butcher shop where my brother worked one time and someone said, 'You're Harold's sister. I can tell because you laugh just like your brother does.'"

Lorraine also was a help to her dad, though she was too young to earn money. "He called me his Powerful Katrinka because once I brought our Christmas tree up some steps he couldn't manage."

All through the years, he wrote cheerful letters home to Sweden, never indicating that he was not well or that things were tough financially. "He was so proud," said Lorraine. "He never did tell his folks he was sick. He didn't want them to know." The family's lack of money meant they had to forego luxuries. "Once the singing group had individual pictures taken and my father couldn't afford to buy one, so years later I bought a print of it. Jim and Kathy had it made into a pencil drawing as a birthday surprise for me. It's over there," she said, nodding toward the portrait on the far wall.

John Wallberg's decline continued and the hot summer of 1936 didn't help his condition. One morning, Lorraine said, her mother couldn't rouse him from his bed and he was taken to Ancker Hospital. Because Lorraine was only 12, she wasn't allowed to visit him when her mother and brother did. "Sometimes he would come to the window and wave to me. I had to wait outside and I don't know how many pairs of shoes I wore out because I would slide down the big cement railings on the side of the hospital's outside steps and the cement wore out the bottoms of my shoes."

John Wallberg died without seeing Lorraine again. "It was December 11, 1936. I will never forget it," she said. He was 47 years old.

Lorraine kept on dancing after her dad's death, and, after she married and Linnea grew old, she and her husband became leaders of the group, learning more than 200 Swedish folk dances, studying in Lindsborg, Kansas, working with folk dancer Gordon Tracie, who came from Seattle several times, and poring over dance videos to figure out the steps in dances. They also helped start new dance groups in Mora and Lindstrom, Minnesota. The dance group performed for the King of Sweden when he visited the Twin Cities in 1976. The McGraths taught Swedish dancing in their basement for years and often hosted dancers from Sweden who came to perform. They just retired from leading the troupe several years ago. "I danced for 67 years with both groups," said Lorraine. And, yes, John Wallberg's daughter is still spinning, as she and her husband continue to dance regularly.

Lorraine's Swedish Meatballs

Lorraine McGrath made twelve pounds of meatballs for her grandson's groom's dinner. Not a one was left over. Don't use the leanest ground beef; Lorraine says a little fat gives the meatballs more flavor. She always grates the onion, too, rather than chopping it. If ground veal is not available use more ground pork rather than more ground beef.

⅓ lb. ground beef
⅓ lb. ground veal
⅓ lb. ground pork
1 egg
1½ tsp. salt
1 small onion, grated
white pepper to taste
½ to ¾ c. bread crumbs
¼ to ½ c. whipping cream
butter for browning

In a large bowl, mix ground meats, egg, salt, grated onion, white pepper and bread crumbs. Add enough whipping cream to make meatballs that are soft, but still hold their shape. Brown in a heavy frying pan. Transfer meatballs to a Dutch oven or heavy sauce pan. Add a little water to the pan, enough to keep the meatballs from burning. Cover and let "steam" over a low heat for about an hour, adding more water if necessary.

Lorraine Wallberg McGrath is justly famous for her cardamom bread. This recipe makes two big loaves, but they won't last long!

Lorraine McGrath's Cardamom Bread

⅓ c. warm water
2 packages dry yeast
1 tsp. sugar, plus another ½ c. sugar
½ c. oil (Lorraine uses canola oil) or ½ c. melted and
    cooled shortening
1 tsp. salt
3 to 3½ heaping tsp. freshly ground cardamom.
1 c. milk, scalded and cooled
3 eggs, plus another egg for top of bread
approximately 5½ c. flour
pearl sugar (large crystals of white sugar made in Sweden
    and available at some grocery stores)

In a small bowl, dissolve yeast in water and add one teaspoon sugar. Stir and set aside until yeast starts to bubble.

Put one-half cup sugar, oil, salt, cardamom and milk in a large bowl and mix well. Add the eggs and mix well again. Add two cups of the flour and the yeast mixture and beat for four minutes at medium speed if using an electric mixer, or one hundred strokes or more if mixing by hand. Add more flour, half a cup at a time, mixing with a spoon, until dough does not stick to spoon handle. Cover and let rest for 15 minutes.

Turn out on floured board and knead. Clean and grease bowl lightly, place bread dough in bowl and let rise, covered, in a warm place until doubled. Punch down, divide in two and form each half into three parts. Make dough "ropes" and braid together, pinching the braid ends together and turning under. Grease two cookie sheets lightly and place one cardamom braid on each sheet. Cover and let rise in a warm place until nearly doubled. In a small bowl, beat egg lightly and brush over tops of bread. Sprinkle with pearl sugar and bake in a preheated 350 oven for 20 to 25 minutes or until tops of braids are golden brown.

Don Carlson
The original Laker

Okay, let's clear up one thing right off the bat: Don Carlson, the first player to be signed for the former Minneapolis Lakers basketball team, doesn't really answer to the name "Swede."

Don "Swede" Carlson was the youngest of four children. The Carlsons lived on Tyler Street in northeast Minneapolis. Photo courtesy of Don Carlson.

"That was a newspaper nickname," said Don's wife, Helene. "I never call him that. He was only half Swedish anyway; his mother was Norwegian," she added. Don was a basketball star at Minneapolis Edison High School in northeast Minneapolis, leading the Tommies to a state title in 1937. "I think he was the only Scandinavian on the team. He was a star. My cousin Willy Warhol played on the same team," said Helene, who answered questions on Don's behalf as he was not well. Don and Helene—whose parents came from Austria but were of Russian ancestry—knew each other in high school, but didn't date until later. Helene played a little basketball herself at Edison. "But not on a team, they didn't have girls' teams then."

Northeast Minneapolis, known more for its Eastern European immigrants, also had a strong Scandinavian element. Don's dad, born in Sweden, and his grandparents settled in northeast Minneapolis. "His grandfather's last name was Grand, but he thought there were too many 'Grands' so he changed it to 'Carlson,'" she said, with a laugh. Don's grandparents emigrated from a town called Stjärna in the province of Östergötland, south of Stockholm, when Don's dad was just three years old. "They paid $93.50 in 1887 for passage from Göteborg for two adults, one child and one infant," Helene said.

When Don was growing up on Tyler Street, his grandparents lived close by and Don was often at their house. His grandparents couldn't speak English. "He used to ask his grandmother for a cookie and she would say 'sluta' to him in Swedish when they were gone. That means 'stop!' but he always thought it meant cookie," she recounted with a laugh. Despite his closeness to his grandparents, Don and Helene have never visited Sweden.

Don Carlson's grandparents, Andrew and Mathilda Carlson, lived near Don's family in northeast Minneapolis. Photo courtesy of Don Carlson.

Don's dad was a foreman at a box factory. "He even learned sign language so he could communicate with the men who couldn't hear," she said.

World War II was on when Don played for the University of Minnesota. He was a star there, too, and the newspapers kept close track of his draft number. "In wartime, everything was so unpredictable. The papers would run stories every week that said, 'probably in two weeks Carlson will be gone.' His number came up and he had to leave in the middle of the season."

In the Air Force, Don trained as a navigator, but the war ended before he saw any action. Don returned to the University, resumed playing and finished his degree in health, physical education and the sciences. "He was surprised later when he found out that a lot of professional players didn't have a college degree. He thought everyone had to have finished college, or they would have nothing to fall back on."

Don's professional career took him out of the state first. Then, when the Laker franchise began, he, along with Tony Jaros, another player who grew up in Minneapolis, was signed by the Lakers. "He was the original Laker. He was playing in Chicago when they signed him," said Helene. Both Don and Tony had previously played with the Chicago Stags of the Basketball Association of America. Don had been the Stags' Most Valuable Player in 1946–47, when the team made it to the top of its division and later lost in the playoff finals to the Philadelphia Warriors.[1]

Don, a forward who was 6-foot, 1-inch, was on the short side for a basketball player even in those years. His teammates, Vern Mikkelsen, at 6–7 and especially George Mikan, who was 6–9, were the big men of the day.

The first Laker game, an away game on Nov. 1, 1947, in Oshkosh, Wisconsin, with the Oshkosh All-Stars, was a triumph for Don. With the score tied, 47–47 with ten seconds to go, he made a field goal to win the game 49–47.[2] Don played for the Lakers for three seasons, and the team won league championships—though for three different leagues—in those years. In 1947–48, the Lakers were in the National Basketball League; in 1948–49, they were part of the Basketball Association of America; and in 1949–50, they belonged to the National Basketball Association.[3]

Don "Swede" Carlson, a star player at Edison High School, was one of the original Laker basketball players. Photo courtesy of Don Carlson.

Don averaged 8.2 points per game the first season, 9.2 during the second and 4.7 the third season. He played in 58, 55, and 57 games respectively during the three years. In the first season, he was third in scoring, after Mikan and Jim Pollard.[4]

The early Lakers were a happy bunch, according to Helene. "They were all his friends. I never heard him say a bad word about any of them. They were all so close. They played as a team, not as individuals. We still see some of them, particularly Vern Mikkelsen."

There was certainly life after basketball for Don. He coached basketball at Columbia Heights High School for 15 years and then became the athletic director there and stayed in that position until his retirement. During the summer, he usually went to summer school. "He went to school practically until he retired. He was always learning." He turned down a chance to coach at the University of Minnesota to stay at Columbia Heights, she added.

The Carlsons had one child, Dawn, who became a figure skater and is now a teacher. While she was at the University, she skated on the ice between periods of the Gopher hockey games. John Mariucci, the late, legendary University of Minnesota hockey coach, used to tease Don and say, " If your daughter had been a boy, she'd be playing hockey," according to Helene. Dawn Carlson Brosseau has two sons—Rick and Matt—who turned out to be baseball players like their dad, not basketball players like their grandfather. Both boys played baseball for the University and Rick now plays in New York state for a farm team of the Toronto Blue Jays. Helene said plenty of teasing went on about the merits of baseball vs. basketball between the boys and their grandfather."

Don built a basketball court in his back yard and the neighbor kids use it from time to time. The fame of a pro basketball player is long-lasting. "He still gets recognized and he still gets requests for autographs. He saved the letters asking for autographs and he must have a stack four or five inches high."

Helene added, "I think it's every little boy's dream to be a professional athlete. And it was a dream realized for him."

Mount Olivet Lutheran Church in south Minneapolis is the largest Lutheran congregation in the United States. Photo courtesy of Mount Olivet.

Chapter Six

Body and Soul

Audrey Grann Johnson
Swedes in stripes

The Swedish Hospital in Minneapolis may be gone physically, but it hardly seems that way to Audrey Johnson and her friends who did their nurses' training there. Audrey and her sister Phyllis followed in their mother's footsteps to get their R.N. degrees at Swedish—Audrey in 1960, Phyllis two years later. The Grann girls and their mom were just three of the 3,054 graduates in the 74 years of the Swedish Hospital School of Nursing.[1]

In early years, the student nurses had to be fluent in both Swedish and English, although that requirement was later dropped. The Hospital, according to its 1902 annual report, was established to serve the Swedish community:

> *"Let it be known that this undertaking is a national one; that it is the Swedish people that are building and managing it; that no particular religious organization or individual is at work; but that it is of the Swedish, for the Swedish people."*[2]

Even when Audrey was there, the Swedish influence could still be felt. "We had lots of Andersons and Johnsons in training, lots of blondes with blue eyes," said Audrey, "and we took care of a lot of old people with Swedish accents." That accent was familiar to Audrey. All four of her grandparents came from Sweden and both of her parents spoke the language fluently. "It was kind of a little Swedish group there [in Worthington]."

Audrey went eagerly from that tight-knit community into the protective, if slightly starchy, arms of the Swedish Hospital, as she had grown up hearing about it from her mother. "It was a very protected place. A lot of us were from small towns. We had housemothers and we got four 12 o'clocks [curfews] a month. If you had an 11 o'clock you couldn't even go to a 9 o'clock movie and get back in time." That didn't mean the girls always followed the rules. "We did sneak in once in a while. There was a certain door by the gym. We'd put a comb in the door to keep it open," said Audrey.

The student nurses had to be early risers. They ate breakfast in the cafeteria in time for devotions at 6:45 A.M. "Then we all scattered and went up to the floors. We got reports from the charge nurse as the shift changed. Then we, and the ones going off duty, sang one hymn together. The patients said they really enjoyed that."

Audrey and the others had their academic classes at nearby Augsburg College, while nurses taught them clinical skills. Mary Chase—a rubberized figure with a big, round face, was a big part of the clinical demonstrations. "She was in the bed when you were taught how to make a bed," said Audrey, "but there were a lot of things you couldn't demonstrate on her." In her off hours, Mary Chase was often put in the strangest places by the students.

The students practiced giving shots—with a saline solution—on each other. "My roommate had to give me a shot and she didn't want to hurt me, so she kept poking me and poking me—it hurt more than if she had just done it quickly," said Audrey.

In the early days of the six-month probationary period, the students were allowed to do simple tasks such as carrying trays to patients. They wore blue-and-white striped uniforms from the start, but didn't get their white caps until the end of the probationary period. "We were capped at six months. We all had 'big sisters' who placed the caps on our heads. We had to kneel down. Our capping took place at First Covenant Church."

"The hardest part of training was that I couldn't be home with my family. Somebody had to work all the time. We had to work weekends and holidays and it was a four-hour drive to Worthington. Sometimes I went home with friends who were from the city."

Traditions and pranks were a big part of the Swedish Hospital experience. "When we got 30 or 40 days from graduation, we'd pin that number of safety pins on our uniform and take one pin off when each day was done. And if a girl got engaged, the others threw her into the swimming pool. On that day, you made sure you had clean underwear," she joked. Audrey got thrown in the pool during her final year—after getting engaged to Bradley Johnson.

Audrey and her friends were not above having a little fun. One day they got up even earlier than usual, stuffed newspaper down knee socks that were inside shoes and sneaked into the bathroom. They carefully set the stuffed shoes and socks in front of the toilets, locked the doors of the stalls from the inside and crawled out from under the doors. Then they waited for the other girls to get up and make a beeline for the bathroom, only to wait and wait for the doors to open.

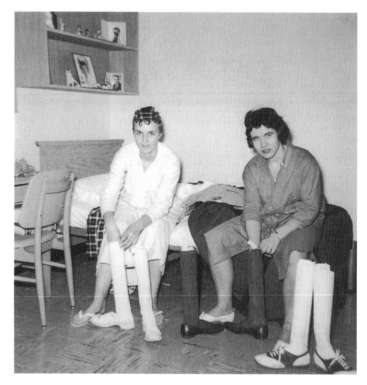

Judy Butler, left, and Betty Johnson helped Audrey Grann Johnson stuff newspapers into knee socks, part of a prank the girls played. Photo courtesy of Audrey Johnson.

Audrey Grann Johnson, left, and Judy Butler locked the toilet stalls and crawled out, leaving the stuffed socks and shoes in front of the toilets. Photo courtesy of Audrey Johnson.

Each year, the graduating student nurses dressed this nude statue in a nurse's uniform. Photo courtesy of Audrey Johnson.

Graduating seniors always decorated the nude statue in front of the late, lamented Charlie's Café with a cap and uniform. The striped student uniforms really got a workout on the traditional "Rip Day". "On the last day you worked, you had your uniform ripped off," said Audrey. A line of the torn uniforms was usually hoisted up on the clothesline, to show the student nurses were leaving their stripes behind.

They may have shed their uniforms, but not their friendships. "I think my class is closer than some," said Audrey. "There were 68 or 70 of us in the class and ten of us get together a lot. We spend the third weekend of August together every year. I could call any of them if I

needed anything. I think being in nurses' training fosters that. You are working with the same people all the time. We eat, sleep, work and play together."

Audrey, who married Dr. Brad Johnson, worked as a nurse for a few years before raising her two boys. She had to choose early between music and nursing as a career. Although nursing won out, she continued to perform and love music. Currently, she is the accompanist for the *Svenskarnas Dag* Girls Choir and has toured Sweden with the choir. She also plays the clarinet in the Robbinsdale city band.

A peek in Sody's diary

Audrey's mother, Mildred Soderholm, who was called "Sody" by her friends in the class of 1930 at Swedish Hospital's School of Nursing in Minneapolis, kept a diary for most of her nurses' training. Sody was a good girl, who was a terrific student and later a wonderful nurse in her hometown of Worthington, Minnesota. Still, she liked to have fun. Judged by the diary entries, she and her friends were always laughing and having a good time. They loved feasting on the boxes of food their families sent and they weren't above hitch-hiking when they had to and sometimes they sneaked in to the dorm after hours. They had crushes on some of the doctors and interns at the hospital and occasionally even on a patient. They were saddened when patients died, but, as they were young and resilient, they soon cheered up and were back to their normal, joyful selves.

Three diary entries show different sides of student nurse life:

"Aug. 8—Oh, for excitement that we had last night! Had 3 deliveries after 3:00 this A.M. Had more fun, too. Had the one that was going to be a breech, but then the kid did a flop . . .

Nov. 30—We requisitioned food for tonight & had a grand spread. Jake [most of the student nurses had nicknames based on their last names] made a big batch of seafoam & I made fudge. Both turned out perfectly . . . "Myja" gave Jake & I three old turkey carcasses & we put them in Eric's bed. She almost threw us out when she discovered them. Oh, but I laughed! . . .

Dec. 11—Dr. Nordin told us some more about the Roentgen Ray tonight [better known as X-rays now]. It's rather hard to understand, I think."

Sody and her pals worked as nurses in Minneapolis for a while after graduation and married one by one. Sody married the man I came to think of—through reading between the lines in the diary—as 'good old Art.' She worked as the chief surgical nurse for the hospital in Worthington and Art farmed. She was tremendously pleased when both of her daughters followed in her footsteps and trained at Swedish. She and all her friends from those happy days in training are gone now, but their blithe spirits live on in the diary, which her daughter now has.

Mildred Soderholm Grann looks solemn but she had a wonderful sense of humor. Photo by Reynolds Studio, courtesy of Audrey Johnson.

Mildred Soderholm Grann, center, was proud that her two daughters, Phyllis, left, and Audrey, right, followed in her footsteps to the Swedish Hospital School of Nursing. Photo courtesy of Audrey Johnson.

Mildred Soderholm Grann was part of the class of 1930 of the Swedish Hospital School of Nursing. Photo courtesy of the Metropolitan Medical Center Historical Library.

Audrey's Rice Ring with Raspberry Sauce

Serves 10–12
1 c. cooked rice
1 pint one-percent milk
½ tsp. salt
1 envelope Knox gelatin
¼ c. cold water
1 pint whipping cream
⅓ c. sugar or more to taste
¼ tsp. almond extract or more to taste

In a saucepan, add milk to the rice and cook over medium heat until thick and creamy. Add the salt and stir. Turn off heat. Dissolve gelatin in one-fourth c. cold water and add to rice. Cool until it begins to set. Whip cream, add sugar and almond extract, mix with rice and place in mold. Refrigerate.

Audrey Johnson's Lutfisk

Yes, here it is, a recipe for the most loved and hated of Swedish foods. It's still a must for many Swedish-Americans on Christmas Eve. There are many who crave it. Others, like Audrey's own husband, say, "If it's so good, how come you only eat it once a year?" Audrey wanted to try selling lutfisk-on-a-stick at the Minnesota State Fair, but couldn't figure out how to keep the slippery stuff on a stick.

lutfisk
white sauce

Rinse lutfisk in cold water. Bake, covered with foil, in a preheated 400 degree F. oven. Check in 20 minutes. If it isn't flaky yet, bake an additional 10 minutes. Serve with a white sauce made with cream.

Raspberry Sauce

Makes a little more than one cup

one 10-oz. package frozen raspberries
1½ tsp. cornstarch
½ c. red currant jelly

Thaw and crush raspberries. Combine raspberries, cornstarch and jelly in a small saucepan. Let mixture come to a boil and cook until thick. Strain and chill. Serve with rice ring.

Swedish Hot Sauce

Audrey Johnson, who has a vast repertoire of recipes and food jokes, gave us this "recipe." Have a glass of water handy.

½ c. plain yogurt
½ c. cottage cheese
½ c. skim milk

Combine and serve. If it's too hot for ya, substitute water for the skim milk.

A Church-going people

Religion played an important role in the lives of many Swedish immigrants. The church was a social as well as spiritual center and many people, once the churches were established, went to services and meetings of church groups several times each week. Many of the early churches branched out and established "daughter" congregations as the Swedes fanned out throughout the metropolitan area. In addition to holding services and sponsoring different committees and groups within the church, many of the early churches—notably First Lutheran in St. Paul and Augustana in Minneapolis—created social outreach services, some of which exist today. Although the majority of Swedes were Lutheran, they also established churches in other denominations—including Covenant, Methodist, Baptist and Episcopalian. Services were in Swedish at first and it took decades for most of the churches to completely switch over to English. Many a battle was fought over the language question.

The first Lutheran church in the territory of Minnesota was First Lutheran, then and now on the east side of St. Paul. It was established in 1854. At first, both Norwegians and Swedes belonged to the church. In 1870 the Norwegians left and the name was changed from "First Scandinavian Evangelical Lutheran Church" to "First Swedish Evangelical Lutheran Church."[3]

Among the pastors was A.P. Montén, who was called to First Lutheran Church in 1877. Montén organized the first Swedish hospital. He had often visited the sick members of his congregation and the 1979 book written for the 125th anniversary of the church quotes him as saying: "I started to think about a new hospital as early as 1878. The need in St. Paul was especially serious, because people from great distances came here for medical attention. It was very difficult for our members to find suitable rooms. Though there were three hospitals in the city, none were acceptable because of the language barrier."[4] Pastor Montén presented a letter about the need for a hospital to the Minnesota Conference in 1880 and the Conference, after discussion, resolved: "The Conference has with joy heard that the First Lutheran Church in St. Paul has commenced in earnest to establish a hospital, and that a society is incorporated that can in a legal way take hold of such work. May their undertaking be realized!" It was realized and Bethesda Lutheran Hospital opened in 1883, treating 71 patients in its first 11 months.[5]

Pastor Montén also established an immigrant home for destitute immigrants and founded a colonization bureau to carry out Swedish colonization work in the Red River Valley. He also bought two Swedish newspapers and combined them, calling the result *Minnesota stats tidning,* The editor was the ubiquitous Eric Norelius.[6]

First Lutheran was among the first of the churches to switch to English language services. Pastor L.A. Johnston, born in the United States (the congregation's first American-born pastor) arrived in 1894 and started an English Bible class in the Sunday School. English services were held on Sunday evenings in 1898 and more were added in 1900. The anniversary book said, regarding Johnston, who resigned in 1904, "He had led the membership into the ways of the twentieth century by introducing the English language into First's pulpit and classroom. He was a wise leader who understood one of the secrets of keeping young people in the membership of the Church."[7]

Several church buildings housed First Lutheran; the current one was finished in 1917.[8] In the 1950s, when many congregations were moving to the suburbs, the congregation voted to stay on the east side, on the edge of Swede Hollow, even though the neighborhood was changing greatly.[9]

Pioneer Lutheran Pastor Eric Norelius and his young wife are pictured in 1855. Photo courtesy of Gustavus Adolphus College.

Eric Norelius
A young man and his blind horse

In May of 1854, a twenty-year-old immigrant, Eric Norelius, preached at a makeshift service at what was to officially become First Lutheran Church in St. Paul, the first Lutheran church in the Twin Cities in the territory of Minnesota. Norelius had come to the United States when he was 17 years old, determined to become a pastor. He was poor, lonely and hungry at times and resisted joining either the Methodists or the Episcopalians because he didn't want to abandon his Lutheran faith, according to *Eric Norelius,* an account of his life written by Emeroy Johnson. A scholarship endowed by Jenny Lind, the so-called "Swedish Nightingale," supported his studies at Capital University in Columbus, Ohio[10] He persevered in his goal to become a pastor and was to become one of the best-known of the early Lutheran pastors in Minnesota, establishing several congregations. He served as a missionary all over Minnesota, driving a sleigh pulled by a blind horse.[11]

His memoir, written in 1897 and translated as *Early Life of Eric Norelius, 1833–1862* by Emeroy Johnson, records his arrival in St. Paul in 1854:

"On May 21, after a six days' journey, we arrived at St. Paul. High and dry, on a natural sandstone cliff lay this lively little city of 6,000 people, a city five years old, looking out upon the then almost unknown world that surrounded it, without any idea of what would some day happen there. It was Sunday afternoon; we met a few of our countrymen at the boat landing . . . They requested me to preach there in the evening . . . The services were held in a primitive schoolhouse on Jackson Street. This street had at that time very few buildings above Seventh Street. Quite a number of people were present, and they seemed happy and cheerful. A few days later Rev. Carlsson came and organized a Scandinavian Evangelical Lutheran congregation, which has been in existence ever since, though it has had to go through many troubles and tribulations."[12]

Pastor William Hyllengren attended Vasa Lutheran Church in Vasa, Minnesota, a village near Red Wing, Minnesota. Photo courtesy of William Hyllengren.

Norelius returned as the first resident pastor for the church in 1860. In the translated account, he writes:

"According to arrangements made by the president of the synod, my family and I were to live in St. Paul and I was to be pastor of the little congregation there and serve it when I was not traveling, and as remuneration for this the congregation would pay my house rent, which was $5.00 per month. In the latter part of October, 1860, I began my work in St. Paul. From my work, "De Svenska Lutherska Församlingarnas Historia," [History of the Swedish Lutheran Congregations] I quote the following regarding the little congregation: 'The congregation was small; it had only thirteen communicant members in the first part of the summer of 1860, but it increased gradually. Peace and harmony prevailed in the congregation and the divine services in the little room were pleasant and refreshing. Mr. John Johnson (a nephew of Rev. Hasselquist) was our song leader, and sometimes he accompanied on a 'psalmodikon.' The celebration of 'julotta' [Christmas service] in 1860 was especially edifying. The lectern was artistically decorated, and the little room beamed bright with candles; but the best thing in the festivities was that the Word of God seemed to be received with joy."[13]

Norelius preached at various places around the Twin Cities and, as the United States entered into the Civil War, he turned up preaching to the troops:

"Later in the summer [1861] troops were being stationed at Fort Snelling to be trained and equipped before being sent south to take part in the war which was then going on. Quite a number of Swedes were enlisted in the various regiments, including many of the members of our congregations. They decided to have our pastors visit them and preach the Word of God to

them . . . In the fall I visited Fort Snelling several times, but I remember especially one time when it was unusually inspiring to preach to our soldiers. In the Third Regiment there was a company that consisted almost entirely of Swedes, but included a few Norwegians, all of whom were very eager to hear me preach to them. They were encamped together with several thousand other men in tents on an open field, and they were busy drilling . . . At a set time in the evening almost the entire Swedish company and also many Swedes from other companies gathered in a plain board shack. A dry-good box was brought in, to serve as pulpit, and a couple of stearin candles were melted fast to the top of it. Some men here and there held candles in their hands. They all stood straight and stiff like real soldiers. Many of them had good voices and some of them were trained hymn singers.

A complete service with liturgy was held, and it touched my heart deeply to hear how they sang the hymns and the responses with spirit and precision. I tried to make my sermon short, but as appealing as possible, and I dare say that I have never in my life had such an audience, nor ever experienced such emotion when preaching the Word. My listeners were all dressed in uniforms and had a manly and soldierly appearance. They would soon be ready to leave for the scene of war. There was seriousness in their eyes, and one could see that the minds of many, perhaps most of them, were deeply stirred. Outside, all around us, camp fires burned here and there, and there were a thousand various noises such as are heard at any army camp. Some pounded with sticks on the walls of our shanty, others crowed like roosters, some sang silly songs to religious melodies, some offered burlesque prayers to ridicule us, etc., etc. If there had been time to report these disturbers of the peace to their commanding officers, they would have been punished, for, after all, religion enjoys protection here in America. But the time did not permit, so we continued our service in cheerful mood, paying no attention to the noises.

I stayed over night with the two lieutenants in their tent, and slept well on a bundle of straw. The next morning the company was drawn up in double column along the camp street, a couple of hymns were sung, and I conducted morning devotions. After wishing them well and pronouncing the benediction upon them, I bade them a hearty farewell. Many of them I was not to see again in this life. "[14]

Norelius was not yet 30 when he preached to the troops, and he went on to live a long and busy life. He died in 1916, after being a pastor for sixty years. He is buried in Vasa, Minnesota, near the church he helped found.

Pastor William Hyllengren preaches occasionally at Vasa Lutheran Church. Photo courtesy of William Hyllengren.

Pastor William Hyllengren
Still serving his master

"Helig, Helig, Helig är Herren Sebaot! Hela jorden är full af hans härlighet. Herren är I sitt heliga temple, hans tron är I himmelen . . ." Pastor William Hyllengren intones as he demonstrates the beginning of the traditional Swedish Lutheran service. He knows the words by heart and sometimes conducts a service in Swedish. "I speak Swedish and once or twice a year I preach in Swedish,

usually in Center City or at *Gammelgården* Museum in Scandia. They have a little chapel at *Gammelgården* [the old farm] that was the first Lutheran church in Minnesota. It still has the original altar."

He is occasionally allowed to wear the well-worn black *prästrock* (priest's coat) that belonged to Eric Norelius, the nearly legendary pioneer Lutheran pastor. "It's in the museum at Vasa," said Pastor Hyllengren, "I'm the only one that they let wear it. It's a little tight on me, but I can get it on." Both men lived in Vasa, a village to the west of Red Wing, Minnesota. Norelius was an early resident and Pastor Hyllengren's grandparents—from Skåne and Småland in Sweden—also settled there. Asked if he had read Norelius' autobiography, Pastor H. laughed and said, "I didn't have to; they lived across from us."

Pastor Hyllengren, second from right, wears Eric Norelius' hat and coat for occasional Swedish services. His second wife, Ruth Hammarberg, is at his left. To his right are Edgar Carlson, former president of Gustavus Adolphus College and Mrs. Carlson. Photo courtesy of William Hyllengren.

Pastor Hyllengren's father was a nephew of Swan Turnblad (see story on the American Swedish Institute), who was the publisher of *Svenska Amerikanska Posten* and had lived in Vasa as a child after emigrating from Sweden. "We called him 'Uncle Swan.' My folks weren't wealthy people and when Uncle Swan came to visit he would shake my mother's hand when he was leaving and press a five-dollar gold piece into her hand."

The Vasa of 1912—when the pastor was born—was a vibrant place, far different from the Vasa of 2001, where the old church is nearly all that remains of the village. "When I was young, there were three churches—a Methodist and a Baptist church in addition to our Lutheran Church. We also had a creamery, a blacksmith shop, two general merchandise stores, a garage, a village school for grades one through eight, an orphanage, a town hall and a shoemaker. You went to Red Wing for a doctor or a dentist. It was a very thriving village, but when cars came, that ended it. They moved the children's home and the Lutheran church is all that is left in Vasa now."

"I was born at home and I spoke perhaps better Swedish than English when I started school. I hear many people say their parents would only speak Swedish when they didn't want them to understand, but that was not the case in my family. There were five of us children; I'm the only one left now."

"The church was my main life and from the time I can remember I wanted to be a pastor. My dad was the custodian of the church. He was the caretaker of the building and he dug graves in the cemetery and mowed the lawn. I helped my dad cut the grass in that cemetery many times."

When Pastor Hyllengren was growing up, the church gradually changed from having all-Swedish services to including English. His Confirmation class was bilingual, with 3 of the 20 confirmands taking instructions in Swedish, at their parents' requests.

He allows himself a little nostalgia for the past: "I was born in the time of horses. On Christmas morning when I was a kid, the farmers would come driving in to the early service with their sleighs and there would be jingle bells on the horses. The men would let the women and children off at the door and then go stable the horses. After the service, they would hitch them up again and pick everyone up and drive off. Today, there are cars in the parking lot."

The children from the Vasa Children's Home would file in and sit together in the front pews of the church for services, he said. And for the Christmas program, the children would be called up to sing or speak their pieces by geographic areas surrounding the church. "They were named after the provinces of Sweden, so we were called up by those names. They would say, "Will the children of Skåne come up? Will the children of Värmland please come up?"

He enrolled at Gustavus Adolphus College after graduating from high school in Red Wing. He was a football star in both high school and college and was a pulling guard on the Gustavus championship team of 1934. He majored in history, took two years of Swedish and met Berenice, the girl who was to become his first wife. "We went together for three years at Gustavus and then I went to seminary for four years and we went together for four more years, because seminary students were not allowed to be married. We got married when I was ordained."

He obtained a bachelor of divinity degree at Augustana Theological Seminary at Rock Island, Illinois, and a master of divinity degree at Chicago Lutheran School of Theology. As an intern in Chicago and as the pastor at St. Paul's Lutheran in Chicago, his duties included occasional preaching in Swedish. He received a call to come to First Lutheran in St. Paul, the first Lutheran Church in the Twin Cities, and served there for four years. And guess who had been one of the first pastors there? None other than Eric Norelius. Pastor Hyllengren and his family, which by then included two children, later moved to Zion Lutheran in Anoka, where he served for 31 years. "I was there until I retired, but I flunked retirement," he said, with a chuckle. "I couldn't handle it. So I've been the visitation pastor here [at Mount Carmel, in northeast Minneapolis] for eleven years. Four days a week I make visits to shut-ins and to people in nursing homes and hospitals. We visit a little and then have devotions and the sacraments. These days it's possible for more people to stay home longer than it had been earlier." Still, he concedes, many of those he ministers to are younger than he is. "Breathing, that's what keeps me alive," he joked. More seriously, he added, "it's doing something, being a part of something."

A world traveler—he has crossed the Atlantic Ocean nine times and the Pacific three times—Pastor Hyllengren was the 1985 recipient of a Distinguished Alumni Citation in the field of religion from Gustavus Adolphus College. During his long career, he has often served as president of organizations, including the Anoka Ministerial Association and Lutheran World Action, Minnesota Synod.

His first and second wives both died years ago and his third wife, Ruth Fardig Hyllengren, is the minister of music at the chapel at Fort Snelling. "We were married two years ago," said Pastor Hyllengren, "but I first met her many years ago when I was at St. Paul's in Chicago.

Gretchen Carlson, Miss America 1989, is Pastor Hyllengren's granddaughter. Photo courtesy of William Hyllengren.

She was 18 years old and had just graduated from high school. I hired her to be the organist for church." Later, Ruth and her first husband moved to St. Paul, where they sometimes visited with the Hyllengrens and always exchanged Christmas cards. "When my second wife died and her husband died, I looked her up." he said.

The pastor's family includes his son, daughter and six grandchildren. He makes special mention of one, Gretchen Carlson, for a reason. "In 1989, she was Miss America. It's more than just a swimsuit contest," he added. The Hyllengrens went to Atlantic City for the pageant and several years later Pastor Hyllengren performed the marriage ceremony for Gretchen and her husband, Casey Close.

Pastor Hyllengren has thought often about the saga of the immigrants. "A lot of them were teenagers who wanted to go to America and most of them never went back. I think about their parents. It must have been possible for them to handle that only because they thought it would be a better place to them. But think of saying farewell to mom and dad and never seeing them again. There had to be a compelling reason for that." He added that many people today criticize current immigrants for sticking together and living close to one another. "They forget that that's what their ancestors did."

Pastor Hyllengren, who has a full head of white hair and a dry sense of humor, looks forward to fall and the *lutfisk*-and-meatball suppers each year. "Every year I find some good place. There's one at Mount Olivet, one at Scandia. They're all very good." He declined to name a favorite. "Oh, no," he said, "I wouldn't want to do that!"

Ten little Youngdahls and how they grew

About one hundred years ago, two Swedish immigrants, both of whom had lost their spouses, renewed old acquaintance and married in 1892. They each had two children from their first marriages—two boys for him, two girls for her. They went on to have six children together. The husband, born Johan Carlsson Ljungdahl—his name was later anglicized to John Youngdahl—and the wife, Elisabeth Matthiasdotter Nelson Ljungdahl, were hard-working, pious people. The family business, a modest grocery store in south Minneapolis, supported the big family. The kids were athletic, talkative, argued among themselves, loved to sing and usually obeyed their parents, according to the engrossing account of the family written by Robert Esbjornson in *A Christian in Politics: Luther W. Youngdahl.*[15]

Luther W. Youngdahl, a former governor of Minnesota and later a judge, is shown with his mother. Photo courtesy of Pastor Jim Anderson.

What are the odds that a couple of these kids would become very successful? Quite possible, perhaps, given native intelligence and lots of hard work. However, the probability of nearly all of them who reached adulthood making a memorable mark on their times is nearly astronomical, right? It happened, though—for these were the Youngdahl children.

For a while, in the 1950s particularly, the Youngdahl name seemed to be everywhere. I was a kid then, but I remember hearing about Gov. Luther Youngdahl, later a judge for the federal district court, who defied the witch hunt mentality regarding any hint of Communism prevalent in the 1950s in the United States.

Kids my age, who were in elementary school in the early days of television, couldn't escape the youngest Youngdahl, Reuben, at lunchtime. Reuben was not only the senior pastor of Mount Olivet Lutheran Church, but he had a short, live TV spot five days a week on WCCO-TV, just before Casey Jones came on. Most days, when we turned the little black-and-white set on, we'd see the tail end of Pastor Youngdahl's talk. He always closed the show, as I recall, with the words, "Live for Today!" I thought of him as sort of a genial opener for Casey and Roundhouse Rodney.

Ruth Youngdahl Nelson was the wife of the Rev. Clarence Nelson. Ruth wrote folksy, uplifting books in addition to assisting her husband with his duties. Never afraid to voice her beliefs, she joined with her son, the Rev. Jon Nelson, and others on Aug. 14, 1982, to make an early morning protest in Puget Sound against the first Trident nuclear submarine. Ruth was arrested, but the charges were later dropped.[16]

Ben Youngdahl was an important man in sociology circles—he was dean of the George Warren Brown School of Social Work at Washington University in St. Louis, Missouri. He was also the family scribe and poet, and penned many a tribute in rhyme to his family.

Oscar was a Republican Congressman from Minnesota, Carl was the director of Augustana College choir in Sioux Falls, South Dakota, Peter was an attorney in Los Angeles, Nora was an artist, Mabel was an activist in the Republican party, and poor little Myrtle died when she was thirteen.

Truly their success as a family is amazing. Pastor Jim Anderson, who is in charge of evangelism and new members at Mount Olivet, tried to explain it. Pastor Jim, who is Mabel Youngdahl Anderson's grandson, knew all the Youngdahls except Myrtle. He said, "The success of the Youngdahls has been attributed to the strength of John and Elisabeth Youngdahl, whose dream was that all their children would be educated. John Youngdahl was well-read and successful. He even judged debates at Washington School near his grocery store. He was poor to start with, but he was a hard worker. The family lived at 1600 11th Avenue South, right near downtown Minneapolis. He rented a store at first, but later he bought his own store at 40th and Lyndale. That was the edge of Minneapolis then. All the children went to church colleges and practically all of his children and grandchildren went to Gustavus."

Even Pastor Jim marvels at his relatives: "Reuben had tremendous charisma. He was like Billy Graham. He was family oriented, very busy; he had a tremendous personality. Luther probably could have been president, but he started showing signs of heart trouble. When Truman appointed him judge, that took him out of a possible Senate race with Humphrey. Ben and Carl were very quiet. Peter, who was divorced, went to California; people used to go to California to start over."

The Youngdahl women were also impressive, Pastor Jim said. "Put Ruth in another generation and she could have been a senator. Her daughter, Mary Nelson, who is head of Bethel New Life, is one of the most powerful women in Chicago. Mabel, my grandmother, was a powerful woman, even though she only had a two-year college degree."

Although most of the Youngdahls called themselves Republicans, they had a decidedly liberal cast, Pastor Jim said. "Today they would be Democrats," he asserted. Luther Youngdahl's decision to drop government indictments in the controversial perjury case against Owen Lattimore was highly controversial, Jim said, and drew an affidavit with an accusation of prejudice from a U.S. Attorney.[17] Youngdahl thundered back that he had taken an oath to preserve the Constitution and that he was striking the affidavit.[18]

Many of the next generation of Youngdahls went into the ministry or other service professions, including Pastor Jim and Pastor Paul Youngdahl, who is now the senior pastor at Mount Olivet. Many of them also moved far away from Minnesota. Pastor Jim and his family spent many years in California before returning to Minnesota. "I think one of the reasons we spread out was the sense that we wanted to prove we could be successful someplace other than Minnesota," Pastor Jim speculated.

The succeeding generation has taken another course. "Our kids are all business people. The helping professions have fallen behind."

The Rev. Reuben K. Youngdahl leads campers into the water. Bernie Vartdal photo, courtesy of Pastor Jim Anderson.

The Youngdahls used to have an annual gathering at Moose Lake, Minnesota, where Mabel and her husband lived. There was always food, fun and music at these meetings and their descendants continue to get together. Ben Youngdahl often wrote poems to commemorate the family. The ten original Youngdahl children are all gone now, but Ben's playful poem—written for a 1965 family reunion—gives a sense of the family solidarity. The "epilogue" is reprinted below:

> *. . . May the numerous members of the*
>   *Youngdahl clan*
> *Give service to others—that is our plan,*
> *In pulpits, in slums, in poverty-sod:*
> *There are many paths that lead to God.*

Mount Olivet
The church that Reuben built

Reuben K. Youngdahl was a young pastor when he got the call to go to Mount Olivet Lutheran Church in 1938. The church, which was established in 1920, had 331 members. Pastor Youngdahl remained at the church until he died, thirty years later. In those three decades, membership soared to nearly 10,000, according to *For Such a Time as This,* a book by Wilfred Bockelman commemorating the church's 75th anniversary.

Since his death, three thousand new members have joined, according to Pastor Jim Anderson, pastor for evangelism and new members and also a cousin of Pastor Youngdahl. Mount Olivet is the largest Lutheran congregation in the United States, according to Pastor Jim.

The sheer numbers of this mega-church mean that despite a sanctuary, side chapels and balcony that hold 2,000 people, latecomers for the nine Christmas services who can't get a seat watch the services on closed-circuit television.

The staff at Mount Olivet is huge, headed by Senior Pastor Paul Youngdahl [Reuben's son], Jim Anderson and eight other pastors, each in charge of specific duties. The pastors alternate preaching on Sundays. Senior Pastor Paul Youngdahl has been at Mount Olivet since his dad's death in 1968, first as associate pastor and since 1974 as the senior pastor.

Mount Olivet isn't just a church. It serves its members and others in many different ways. The congregation dedicated Mount Olivet Home, with rooms for 96 residents, in 1960. In 1965, Mount Olivet Careview, a nursing home, was established, and Mount Olivet Rolling Acres, which cares for disabled children, opened its doors in 1969. Cathedral of the Pines, the church's beloved summer camp near Lutsen, Minnesota, hosted its first overnight visitors in 1949 and attendance quickly grew; each summer, more than 2,000 campers attend the summer sessions. Among Mount Olivet's other ministries are a retreat center and Mount Olivet Day Services.

Renee Weberg Gillespie is shown on her fifth birthday holding a doll. Photo courtesy of Renee Gillespie.

Chapter Seven

The Next Generations

Although there is still a trickle of new arrivals from Sweden to the Twin Cities, the huge immigration has been over for many decades and many of those who identify with Sweden are now three, four or even five generations removed from the land their ancestors left. Indeed, in many cases Sweden is just one of several countries from which their forebears hailed. While some don't pay any attention to their ancestry, others cultivate it zealously. Most of us fall somewhere in between the two extremes. Often, the tender ties between children and their Swedish grandparents or great-grandparents are cherished reminders that we were all once from someplace else.

Renee Weberg Gillespie
A little girl just like grandma

Every Christmas, Renee Weberg Gillespie pauses in her holiday preparations in her town house in Arden Hills north of St. Paul and takes out the book Grandma Weberg gave her. The book, *Elle Kari,* is about a little girl who lived in Northern Sweden and had a pet reindeer. Renee doesn't know much more about the story, because it is in Swedish and she can't read the language of her father's ancestors. The book is one of her treasures, however. "I think it was a Christmas present. I would sit next to grandma, because she was too old for me to sit on her lap, and she read it to me and told me what it was about. She said it was like when she was a little girl in Sweden, except that she was from a different place. And she said the little girl was just like me, too. I like to hold the book now. It makes me feel close to her."

When Renee's grandma was a little girl in Sweden, she didn't have a pet reindeer, but she did live on an island called Sollerön in Lake Siljan near the town of Mora in the province of Dalarna, the most Swedish of all provinces, some say. Her name was Anna Olsson and she was born in 1874. She lived with her father and mother, Anders and Maria Nelsson Olsson, and her sister Carin, who was four years older than she was, and brothers Olaf, Andrew and Nels. The island residents went to church in Mora, across the lake. They used long, narrow boats that looked like Viking ships to transport them across the lake to the church. The boats held up to 25 or 30 people, according to Renee's dad's cousin, the late Ted Flodquist, and each person had an oar to help row the boat. Today, the church boats can still be seen on Lake Siljan, but they are now used in rowing competitions.

Because the island was farmed and there was little room for pastures, families who had cows sometimes had them rowed across the lake to roam the mountain pastures. Every three days, a milking crew went over to the mountain to milk the cows, make cheese and bring the butter back to town. Since the cattle wandered freely over the mountain pastures, a horn blower would sound a long horn to call the cows. Anders Olsson's sister, Margit, was a horn blower and she caught the eye of Anders Zorn, one of Sweden's best-known painters. Zorn lived in Mora and he painted Margit in a work titled simply "Horn Blower." The painting is in the Zorn Museum in Mora today. Renee has been told that she resembles the girl in the painting—her great-great aunt.

Anna Olsson came to Minnesota with her family in 1883 when she was eight or nine years old. The family settled in Isanti County, north of the Twin Cities. Anna married Martin Weberg (also spelled Wiberg) in 1893, the same year her beloved sister Carin married Carl Oscar Flodquist. Both the bridegrooms were Swedish immigrants. Their oldest brother, Olaf Olsson, never learned to read English, although his sisters could. Ole worked as a carpenter and was a strong union man. Renee has a silver snuffbox that belonged to him. His name, spelled "O. Olson," is engraved in the lid. Ole played the violin and his younger brother, Andrew, not only played the violin but made violins until his dad made him stop. Anders Olsson broke his son's violins, saying they were the instruments of the devil and encouraged dancing.

The youngest Olsson sibling, Nels, had a varied career. He was a carpenter and cabinetmaker in Minneapolis and was also a professional boxer. Although deaf since childhood, he performed as a magician. His wife was also deaf and they got along with the help of a "hearing" dog, who was trained to alert them when the phone or doorbell rang.

Through the years, Anna and her sister, Carin re-

Anna Olsson and Martin Weberg, Renee Weberg Gillespie's grandparents, were both Swedish immigrants. They married in November, 1893. Photo courtesy of Renee Gillespie.

mained very close. They were married the same year and also died in the same year—1965. "They looked alike and when they were together they were always holding hands and whispering to each other. They may have been in their eighties, but they acted like they were five years old," said Renee.

Grandma Weberg was pleasant, but her husband, Martin, was gruff, according to the family legend. "He was very stubborn and he chewed snuff all the time. I remember sitting on his lap and he would run his fingers over our heads to see if we had big brains." He was a horse trader by profession and never learned to drive. The Webergs lived in Minneapolis first, then returned to Isanti County and finally settled for good on Willow

Avenue in north Minneapolis. Anna spoke, wrote and read English well, but Martin never learned it.

Anna and Carin each had several children who lived to grow up—among them were Renee's dad, Milt, and his cousin, Ted Flodquist. Ted had an older brother, Carl, who was a strong union man and the family didn't always appreciate his stand. "He was always talking about politics. He was very active in the union. My mom [Ruth Chrislock Weberg] was a very independent thinker and Carl would stop by and have coffee with her and talk about the union when my dad was working 24-hour shifts at the fire station. The last time I saw Carl he was at an anniversary party and he said to me, 'Why didn't you go to the National Women's Conference? What is wrong with you?'"

Renee has an older brother and sister, Ron and Regina (Jeannie) and they grew up first in north Minneapolis and later northeast. "When my mom had her babies, Grandma Weberg would come and stay. And every year my parents would go deer hunting and she'd come and stay and make rye bread and darn all my father's socks."

There was a downside to grandma's visits, however. "When we found out she was coming, my sister and I would fight over who would get to sleep on the couch instead of sharing a room with grandma. We knew she would keep us awake praying all night in Swedish. She'd start out by saying "Lordy, Lordy, Lordy" in English and then whisper prayers in Swedish. It was haunting."

Renee Weberg Gillespie's Grandma Weberg made this rye bread when she came to stay with the Webergs. The v-shaped cuts on the top are not strictly necessary, but you should do as grandma did if you really want this bread to be authentic. It makes two round loaves.

Grandma Weberg's Swedish Rye Bread

2 c. milk, scalded and cooled to lukewarm
1 package dry yeast
¼ c. very warm, but not hot, water
¼ c. butter, softened or melted
½ c. molasses
½ c. brown sugar
½ tsp. salt
3 c. medium rye flour
3 to 4 c. white flour

Scald milk and cool. In a large bowl, dissolve yeast in warm water. When it starts to bubble (up to five minutes), add the cooled milk, butter, molasses, brown sugar and salt and stir well. Add the rye flour and mix well. Add the white flour, half a cup at a time, until the dough is fairly stiff, but still workable. Let rest fifteen minutes, covered. Turn out on a floured surface and knead for about six minutes, adding flour sparingly. Clean and grease bowl slightly with oil and put dough in bowl, turning it over to grease the top. Let rise in a warm place until doubled. Punch down and form into two round loaves. Flatten slightly on top and place in round nine-inch cake pans or other round pans. Let rise until almost doubled. With the point of a very sharp knife, make several rows of little v-shaped cuts on the top of each loaf. Do not cut far into the surface. Bake in a preheated oven at 350 degrees until the loaves sound hollow when tapped (about 30–40 minutes, though times will vary with different ovens.)

Gretchen Carlson
Growing up Swedish

Gretchen Carlson is a fifth generation Swedish-American, but she holds fast to her heritage, thanks in part to the diligence of her grandpa, Pastor William Hyllengren. Pastor Hyllengren, who served Zion Lutheran Church in Anoka for more than 31 years, is still Gretchen's mentor in Swedishness and in the art of telling jokes aimed at the Norwegians.

"When we were kids we were so proud to say that we were one hundred percent Swedish. It was a huge deal.

Gretchen Carlson's grandfather, William Hyllengren, was in the audience when she was chosen Miss America 1989. Photo courtesy of William Hyllengren.

My grandparents fostered that. A lot of my childhood memories relate to being Swedish. We lived only a mile or so from our grandparents and we would stay overnight a lot. They would speak Swedish together and I would always say, 'Grandpa, you have to tell me what you were talking about!' They had devotions every morning in Swedish. Being Swedish remains a big part of my life even now, with the traditions and the foods. Grandpa loves food and the story is that you always know where you can find him in November and December because he's at all the *lutfisk* and meatball church suppers. He loves it. There's no way he could overdose on that stuff."

Around the table, Gretchen said, her grandpa was a great joke-teller. "He'd be sitting there and then he'd start telling those jokes. Usually the Norwegians were the bad guys and the Swedes were the good guys." Of course, you could tell it the other way, too.

Grandpa was there for Gretchen always. He went to Atlantic City when she was in the Miss America Pageant in 1989, which she won [Yay for the Swedes!]. Gretchen was the first Miss America to play a classical violin piece in the talent competition. She even managed to inject a bit of her heritage into the pageant. A photo of the two—Gretchen and grandpa—shows them both smiling the same wide smile. Gretchen wears a white dress, with a crown of pink-and-white flowers in her hair and around her shoulders.

"There is a parade during the pageant and each person is supposed to wear something that reflects her heritage. The dress I had on is modeled after a dress worn during summer festivals in Sweden," she said.

Gretchen had brains as well as beauty and talent. She won a scholarship to Julliard in New York and studied at

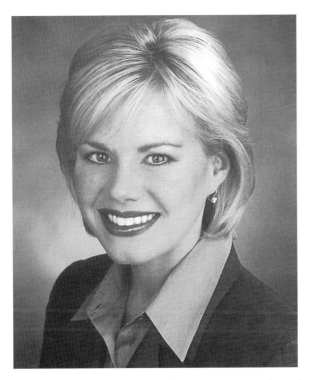

Gretchen Carlson is currently a correspondent for CBS news in New York City. Photo courtesy of Gretchen Carlson.

Oxford in England while she was an undergraduate at Stanford University in California. Now, after working at several regional television stations, she is a correspondent for CBS news in New York and travels around the world on assignment.

Several years ago, she married Casey Close, who—oh, dear—is not Swedish. "Before that, grandpa kept saying to me, 'Can't you find a man who's Swedish?'" Gretchen said with a laugh. When the two married, there was grandpa, front and center, performing the ceremony.

Barbara Flanagan Sanford
Another secret Swede

As a longtime newspaper columnist, Barbara Flanagan has been the voice of civic consciousness, though she calls herself a nag. And, for decades, she's written about big names in the Twin Cities and still bigger names passing through town. She's led her readers on vicarious visits to Europe a dozen times and she is recognized regularly. Yes, everybody knows Barbara Flanagan, but it may come as a surprise that she is what I call "a secret Swede." That's stretching a point, as it's no real secret that she's one-fourth Swedish, but her Irish last name and her red hair have typecast her, as surely as my name has me.

To talk about her heritage and her career in general, we met, for the first time since we worked together on the old *Minneapolis Star* thirty years ago, at Peter's Grill in downtown Minneapolis. Barbara has written about the Grill often and it was convenient for her to meet for a sandwich after her workout at a downtown gym. She was already established and writing her column, which alternated with Jim Klobuchar's, when I did my four-year stint at the *Star* before precipitously quitting to work on a dairy farm in Norway—yes, really! Three decades after I left, Barbara continues to write her column, though it's now monthly. "I just nag away," she said. "It's nice to be able to do it once a month." The column appears in the *Minneapolis StarTribune* on the first Monday of each month.

Of course, we spent some time talking about old times while we ate. She was amused when I apologized to her for the *Star's* promotion department's long-ago billing of me as the first woman sports writer on the staff. I felt a little sleazy as I knew she had done a little

Barbara Flanagan's grandmother, Alma Agnes Lund Barnes, whose parents were from Sweden, moved to Minneapolis to be with Barbara. This photo was taken in 1967, on Alma Barnes' 88th birthday. Photo courtesy of Barbara Flanagan Sanford.

sports writing herself long before I showed up. "Yes, I did do some sports writing, but I wasn't on the sports staff the way you were. When I worked on the *Minneapolis Times,* Dick Cullum had me do a story about women's sports once or twice a week. I still remember interviewing a woman's heavyweight wrestling champion. Her name was Mildred Burke."

Cullum chose his writer well. Barbara, who grew up in Des Moines, Iowa, was not only a sports fan, but a participant—something I never was. "I grew up loving sports. I loved the St. Louis Cardinals. I went to all the games in high school and I played sports, too. I ran track in high school. Of course, that was big in Des Moines, because of the Drake Relays [an annual track meet held at Drake University, Barbara's alma mater]."

As a full-time sportswriter, I might have covered more sports than she did, but I didn't get to interview Ginger Rogers, Cary Grant ("I loved Cary Grant," said Barbara), Marlon Brando ("I had a great lunch with him"), Charlton Heston, Judy Garland ("I was just fascinated with Judy Garland") Rosalind Russell ("She was great") or Joan Crawford ("She was awful"). Nor did I travel any further than Wyoming, for a ski meet. Barbara, on the other hand, was often on the move. She went to Paris to

134

cover fashion shows, to Italy to see the Pope, and to Europe to cover the beginning and the end of General Lauris Norstad's term as NATO chief.

Her first trip abroad, in 1949, was to Sweden. "I was the first member of our family to go back to Sweden. I went for Lucia Day for the *Tribune*. The American Swedish Institute and SAS [the Scandinavian airline] got together and picked five girls from across the country to go to Sweden for Lucia Day [December 13th]. We all had to get up very early in the morning and all the girls wore the white gowns and wreaths with burning candles on their hair. I was a nervous wreck on the trip, but it was an incredible event. I didn't grow up knowing about it. I've been to Sweden three times now, but I never have pursued where my great-grandparents came from."

In her years as a general assignment reporter, she wrote many stories that had a Swedish element. "I used to cover *Svenskarnas Day*. In its heyday, it was really something. When the king and queen of Sweden came, I got the only official interview with them. He was quiet and didn't say much and she was very vivacious."

Her family's Swedish heritage was not a big factor in Barbara's life. Her great-grandparents, Sven and Ida Marie Lund, were almost accidental immigrants. "Her dad was a soldier to the king and he went to law school. They came to America on their honeymoon to see friends and my great-grandmother loved it so much she refused to go back to Sweden." They settled in Iowa and Sven Lund became a prosperous farmer and county commissioner and quickly adopted American ways, though vestiges of his Swedish culture still remained. His wife always had hired girls from Sweden to do the housework and the notice of his daughter's Alma's wed-

ding to Canadian Walter Barnes [the two were to be Barbara's beloved grandparents] appeared in a Chicago Swedish-language newspaper.

As an old man, her great-grandfather taught tiny Barbara the old Swedish habit of dunking anything resembling bread in morning coffee. "We used to go for walks together. One thing I remember is that he taught me how to dunk things in coffee and when I was in preschool the teacher went around the class asking everyone what they had for breakfast and I said, 'Cereal, milk and coffee.'"

Barbara grew up in an extended family. Her mother and father divorced when she was young and she and her mother lived with Walter and Alma Barnes in Des Moines. "They were terrific," she said. "I actually kind of had two mothers. The three of us [Barbara, her mother and her grandmother] did a lot together. We'd go out and go to movies while my grandfather stayed at home. Once we went to Chicago on the train."

Her mother, Marie Barnes Flanagan, Barbara said, was "an entrepreneur. She had a dancing academy." Although her great-grandparents were determined to be American, her grandmother sometimes spoke to her sisters in Swedish on the telephone, particularly when she didn't want Barbara to overhear.

Barbara's "Swedish grandmother," as she often referred to her in her newspaper column, came up to Minneapolis with Barbara when she started a summer job working for the *Minneapolis Times* newspaper here at the tender age of 18. The two came back the following summer, after Barbara completed a year at Drake and they remained here while Barbara pursued her career. "My grandmother was always a supporter of what I did." In later years, Barbara married Earl Sanford and became an instant mother to his three children. The two now have three grandchildren.

Does she ever wonder what to write about, I asked. She rolled her eyes and laughed that wonderful, throaty laugh of hers. "I've never been at a loss for words and I've had as good a career as anyone could hope to," she said. And, of course, it's not over yet. Long may she write!

The late Prince of Bertil of Sweden, left, and Wendell Anderson in 1975. Photo courtesy of the American Swedish Institute.

Grandmother's Swedish Pancakes

Barbara Flanagan's grandmother made these pancakes occasionally. Barbara watched her grandmother make them and wrote down what she did. Makes four large pancakes, or, if you want to make them smaller and easier to turn, six to eight.

2 eggs
2 c. milk
½ tsp. salt
2 tsp. sugar
1 c. flour
½ c. Bisquick or an additional half cup flour
butter or oil for frying

In a medium bowl, beat the eggs. Add the milk and beat some more, then add the salt and sugar and continue beating. Add the flour, little by little, beating after each addition. The batter will be thin. Heat a small amount of butter or oil in a large skillet and pour one-fourth of the batter in at a time. Fry on both sides. Serve spread with butter, rolled up and topped with maple syrup or serve for dessert with fruit or whipped cream.

Wendell Anderson
From the east side to the king's side

Wendell Anderson (Yes, THAT Wendell Anderson—Olympic hockey player, former governor and senator and current honorary consul for Sweden) used to be just another Swedish kid from the east side of St. Paul. True, he grew up long after the Swedes had left Swede Hollow, but there was still a strong Swedish strain among the multi-cultural area, which included Irish, Polish and Italian kids as well as Swedes.

The kids could tell each other's ethnic background from the church they attended, he said. "If you were Polish, you went to St. Casimir's. If you were Irish, you went to St. Patrick's. If you were Italian, you went to St. Ambrose's." And Wendell—let's call him Wendy, because everyone else does—went to Messiah Lutheran because he was Swedish.

In fact, Wendy is very Swedish: all four of his grandparents came from Sweden. His mother's parents settled just east of Swede Hollow, close to the streetcar barn, and his dad's father, who came to the U.S. in 1892, lived first in a boarding house and livery stable on Seventh and Robert Streets in St. Paul. His grandfather soon sent for his fiancée, their baby and his future mother-in-law. Wendy is still angry for their sake when he tells their story: "My grandfather was 17 when he got my grandmother pregnant. She was 16. The Lutheran priest wouldn't marry them because she was pregnant. Isn't that terrible? So they came here and they got married and had ten more children." The relatives on his dad's side, he continued, never talked much about Sweden.

His paternal grandparents moved out to a farm in what was then rural Ramsey County. "I was probably there most Sundays." he said. "They were very poor, very modest people."

Wendy was the middle one of three brothers. Their dad worked in a packing house and the kids went to work early, especially in summer. "When I was 12 years old, I worked eight hours six days a week at a truck farm, picking tomatoes and cabbages. I made 30 cents an hour. I made $14.80 a week."

Wendy went to Johnson High School in St. Paul. Coincidentally, the school's sports nickname is "the governors," named after an earlier governor, John A. Johnson. There and later at the University of Minnesota, he played defense on the hockey teams. He went on to

Wendell Anderson played hockey for Johnson High School, the University of Minnesota and for the United States in the 1956 Olympics in Cortina, Italy. Courtesy of the University of Minnesota.

play for the U.S. in the 1956 Olympics in Cortina, Italy. The team won the silver medal, losing to the Russians.

Hockey didn't end with the Olympics. When we spoke, he said, "I just finished the hockey season. It's a group of old men keeping it up." But, much as he liked sports, what Wendy really wanted to do was to be in politics. Why politics? Surprised to be asked, he replied,

"Well—some people like to play the piano, I liked politics and government." He followed up his degree in history with a law degree, both from the University of Minnesota and he was elected to the Minnesota House of Representatives while still in law school and just 25 years old. He was later elected to the state senate and eventually, after 12 years in the legislature, was elected governor when he was just 37 years old. At that time, he was younger than any other governor in the U.S.

Wendy may have been the youngest governor, but he was far from the only Swede. "Governors of Minnesota 1849–1971" which has an introduction by Russell R. Fridley, former director of the Minnesota Historical Society, notes that Luther Youngdahl was Swedish on both sides and Floyd B. Olson, and Orville Freeman were Swedish and Norwegian. All three were born in Minneapolis. Other governors of Swedish descent— including Elmer L. Andersen, Arnie Carlson and Harold Levander—weren't born in the Twin Cities, but have spent many years here. Several early governors were also Swedish.[1]

Wendell Anderson was appointed to serve in the U.S. Senate in 1977–78, but lost in the next election, which abruptly returned him to private life after years in the public eye. Does he miss politics? "I did miss it at first, but I don't now," he said.

Back in law practice for 11 years now, he also serves as the honorary consul general of Sweden. It's a part-time position, sometimes very busy, with a flurry of meetings to arrange and dignitaries to meet—and sometimes quiet. "It's normally very interesting work and fun," he said. Being the honorary consul general has given Wendy a greater appreciation for the country his grandparents left. "Stockholm I believe is the most beautiful city in Europe and Sweden is an incredibly successful country. There is just about a 100 percent literacy rate and for more than sixty years women have been treated with equal rights."

Although he doesn't speak Swedish well ("I've never said anything in Swedish that any Swede could understand," he said wryly), he loves the country and considers visiting it his hobby. "I went to Sweden while I was governor and we discovered we had a significant number of relatives there. We're very close to them. When I was younger I didn't have a chance to go there as often, but now I've been there 36 times, mostly in the last 15 years. I go there because I want to go there. I even like being there in the winter if the sun is out."

He has three grown children—two daughters and one son. When he's not working or visiting his kids, you might find him doing something athletic. In addition to playing hockey, he enjoys tennis and golf. What about fishing? The famous photo of him on the cover of *Time* magazine showed him hauling in a big fish, after all. Wendy gave a short laugh: "I'm too young to be a fisherman," was his response.

Chapter Eight

For a Swedish Accent

Even now, when most of the old-timers are gone, there are touches of Swedish culture to be found in the Twin Cities. As in most hyphenated American cultures, the traditional food outlasts the native language by several generations. Well before Christmas, there are reminders that the Swedish-Americans are still here. Many churches have annual *lutfisk* and meatball suppers. From September on, it is a succession of suppers, a little like a progressive dinner with only two entrees. Some *lutfisk*-lovers follow their noses all during late fall.

In summer, dedicated Swedes and those who just like to have a good time are apt to show up at the *Midsommar Dag* (Midsummer Day) celebration at the American Swedish Institute to dance around the Maypole, and—usually a week later—they gather again in Minnehaha Park in south Minneapolis for *Svenskarnas Dag* (the Swedes' Day). The day-long party in the park has been an annual event since 1934, although earlier celebrations of a similar type were held at Phalen Park in St. Paul.

At Christmas, even families that no longer think of themselves as anything but American reveal their roots by their customs and their foods. My family—like most Scandinavians here—has always had a celebration on Christmas Eve. We have ham, potato sausage and meatballs, often herring (though there are few takers), and

lots of other things. Sometimes there is rice pudding, which my mother used to make. Once in a while, I've made *sillsallad* (herring salad) according to a verbal recipe handed down from my great-grandmother. I always contribute a loaf of *limpa* (Swedish rye bread) to the meal.

You will notice I didn't say we eat *lutefisk* or, as the Swedes write it, *lutfisk*. We tried that a couple of times and it didn't go over very well. Years ago we made *glögg*, a warm red wine loaded with almonds and raisins, and I think it may be time to revive the tradition. We always opened our presents on Christmas Eve and then had stockings to open the next morning. My English husband's family always opened presents on Christmas Day. We compromised and do a bit of both.

Nu är det jul igen

If baking is only done once a year, it is done for Christmas and many of the third- and fourth-generation wouldn't dream of a Christmas without *spritz* cookies or *limpa* (Swedish rye bread) and some brave souls still make Swedish potato sausage, *sylta* and other seasonal specialties. Most Swedes cheat and get the store-bought versions at Ingebretsen's or Ready Meats in Minneapolis.

Jessica Greupner, center, was the 1995 Lucia at the American Swedish Institute. Her attendants were Alexandra (Alix) Lewis, left, and Annette Öster. Photo courtesy of the American Swedish Institute.

But food isn't the only Swedish tradition still celebrated at Christmas time. A couple of Lutheran churches still offer Christmas services either in Swedish or with Swedish touches. And, at the American Swedish Institute, the annual Christmas bazaars feature crafts and homemade goodies. Also, the dining room and four other rooms reflect Christmas in Sweden and four other Nordic nations—Norway, Denmark, Finland and Iceland. Tables in the rooms are set with the beautiful china and crystal, with linen napkins folded in fancy shapes and a wonderful centerpiece. In the dining room, always the Swedish room for Christmas, a tree near the window has traditional Swedish decorations, including the fringed, candy filled *karameller*.

And then, there is Lucia Day, December 13th. There may be several places around the Twin Cities to see the Lucia procession, but perhaps the most dramatic procession is at the American Swedish Institute. Although the Institute has one or two afternoon performances of the procession and program, it is worth joining the Institute to be able to attend the early morning one. The old legend holds that Lucia, who was actually a saint from Sicily, is a symbol of light for darkest Scandinavia. How she wound up as a symbol of the holiday season in a country more than one thousand miles away from Italy is beyond me.

In Minnesota, any hope of longer, warmer days coming again is worth following up. And so, muffled- and mittened-up members of the Institute trickle into the Grand Hall shortly before seven a.m., well before any light shows in the sky. Usually, too, the temperature is way, way down. This is a good time to think about the light coming at the end of winter.

Just before seven, all lights in the place are turned off. People wait in silence, ears straining to catch the first words of the haunting old song as its young singers make their way slowly down from the third floor. The littlest girls in the choir and the gingerbread boys and girls come first, carrying electric candles. The crowd on the second floor balcony parts to let them through as they wander from room to room, singing the song again and again. Then come the white-robed attendants, wreaths in their hair. The girl chosen to be the Lucia wears a white gown with a red sash and her hair is crowned with a wreath of boxwood leaves set with seven white electric candles, their glow piercing the darkness. It is a beautiful, moving procession; I shivered with delight the first time I saw and heard it. The choir stands on the grand staircase, singing several more songs. Then everyone—choir, Lucia, attendants and the listeners—adjourns to the auditorium for a short program, including a sing-along of Swedish Christmas songs, and then we eat special Lucia refreshments—ginger snaps *(pepparkakor)* and Lucia buns *(lussekatter)*, with coffee, of course. And then it is over and the Christmas season has indeed begun.

Lussekatter

(Lucia buns)

This recipe is also one of Gunhild Anderson's. It makes about four dozen buns.

1 package active dry yeast
¼ c. warm water
¾ c. milk
½ c. butter or margarine
½ c. sugar
2 eggs
¼ tsp. salt
¼ tsp. powdered saffron, dissolved in a half teaspoon of
 very hot water.
4 c. flour
raisins
for the egg wash:
 one egg
 2 tbsp. water

In a large bowl, dissolve yeast in warm water and set aside until yeast starts to bubble. Meanwhile, warm the milk in a small saucepan, but not to the boiling point. Turn heat off and let butter melt in the milk. Add the milk, butter, sugar, eggs, salt, saffron, and two cups of flour to the yeast. Mix for three minutes if using a mixer, or stir by hand. Add the remaining two cups of flour by hand, using a wooden spoon. Turn out on a floured board and let rest 15 minutes. Knead until smooth and shiny. Add a little more flour if needed for easy handling.

Wash the bowl out, grease it slightly, put the dough in and let rise until doubled in bulk. Turn out on floured board and pinch off portions, roll between hands into ropes of dough and shape into *lussekatter*—traditional "S" shapes are perhaps the most popular. Let buns rise on a cookie sheet until nearly doubled. Combine egg and water and brush over tops of *lussekatter*. Place a raisin in the center of each curve of the "S." Bake for 10 minutes at 450 degrees.

Pepparkakor

(ginger cookies)

This is Gunhild Anderson's recipe for the ginger cookies beloved by Swedes. They are often cut in heart shapes, with a bit of almond in the center of each heart. These ginger cookies and the Lucia buns are traditionally served on the morning of Lucia Day, December 13. The oldest daughter in the family serves them to her parents just at daybreak.

3½ c. flour
1 tsp. baking soda
½ tsp. salt
¾ tbsp. ginger
2 tsp. cinnamon
2 tsp. cloves
½ c. dark corn syrup
1 c. butter
1 c. sugar
1 egg

Mix flour, soda, salt and spices together. Heat syrup until warm (not boiling). Melt the butter and sugar in syrup, stirring to dissolve the sugar. Add egg. Combine dry and liquid ingredients. Put in a cool place overnight. Roll out on floured surface and cut in desired shapes. Place on greased cookie sheet and bake at 375 for 10 minutes.

Great-grandma's Herring Salad

My mother, Eleanor Anderson Gillespie, told me about the herring salad my great-grandmother, Christine Anderson Petersen, made every Christmas Eve in Red Wing, Minnesota. Grandma Petersen emigrated from Dalsland, Sweden with her dad when she was 13 years old. He worked as a lumberjack in the woods in Wisconsin and she was a hired girl. The rest of the family followed later. This recipe is not written down and amounts are what you prefer. First, hard boil eggs and boil some potatoes. Cut both up in small pieces. Chop pickled herring into bite-sized pieces. Chop an onion and some pickled beets up, too. Arrange all of these ingredients in concentric rings on a platter. Sprinkle a little salt and pepper over them. Pour cream (sweet or sour) over or leave plain.

Aunt Aggie's Spritz Cookies

My mother's dearly loved cousin Jean Ross gave me this recipe for the cookies their Aunt Agnes Petersen made each Christmas in Red Wing, Minnesota.

1 c. butter
½ c. sugar
3 egg yolks
2 tsp. almond extract
2 c. plus 1 tbsp. unsifted flour

Mix all ingredients together and put through a cookie press. Bake 8–10 minutes in a preheated 375 degree oven.

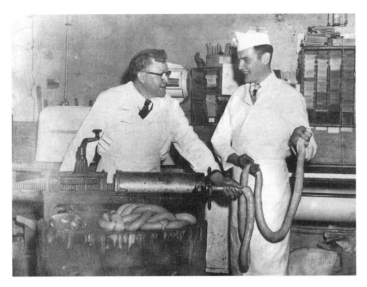

Warren Dahl, right, is shown some years ago making Swedish sausage, one of Ingebretsen's best-selling items at Christmas time. Ingebretsen's doesn't give out its recipe. Photo courtesy of Ingebretsen's.

The Great Swedish Sausage War

Maybe we shouldn't call it the Great Swedish Sausage War. But then again, all the makers of Swedish potato sausage dig in and insist that theirs is the best recipe for the Christmas treat. In this three-corner sausage meet, we have Marci Elfstrom Osborne, Ann-Christine Moonen and Dave Carlson. All are true Minnesota Swedes: Marci's grandfather was from Värmland, Ann's mother was from Sweden and Dave describes himself as Swedish and Norwegian.

Marci's mother, my dearly beloved neighbor, Phyllis Johnson Elfstrom, whose story is elsewhere in this book, made the sausage every year. She stuffed the sausage into casings using a small angel food pan turned upside-down. Other people hold the casing onto the end of a meat grinder and force the meat mixture into the casing that way. Ann uses the meat grinder and also—harking back to the old days in Sweden—part of a cow horn from Sweden, which is more than one hundred years old. It acts as a funnel for the meat.

Love and remembrance aren't among the ingredients listed in Ann's sausage, but they are present nonetheless. "The recipe is from my great-aunt Kristine, who came over from Värmland, Sweden, in 1910. My mother was the one who followed her around measuring the ingredients, because Kristine didn't measure them." Ann's mother made the sausage until her death several years ago and now Ann, with the help of several friends, is the sausage maker.

Ann goes into the sausage-making mode the week before Christmas and also in summer for an annual family reunion. She is joined by one or more of a trio of friends—Mariann Tiblin, Jean Anderson and Karen Osterbauer. Mariann, a native of Sweden, first started making the sausage with Ann's mother and continues to help with the holiday tradition. Making the sausage can't be hurried. "It's an all-afternoon thing," said Ann. "You have to allow plenty of time to do it." Coffee and cookies help the sausage makers keep up their strength.

As she makes the sausage, Ann said, she feels a strong connection with the past. "My mother is all around us when we're making it and I'm sure she is very proud, and my dad, too. Kristine was his aunt and he would be happy that I'm carrying on the tradition." Ann's mother, Gunvor Johnson, was born and raised in Sweden and her father, though born in the United States, spent part of his early years there. Ann is bilingual and was raised in St. Paul and Minneapolis with lots of Swedish food to eat and plenty of artwork on the walls of her home. "I realized when I went to other people's houses that I had more of a European home," she said.

In addition to working part-time, Ann leads tours of the metropolitan area and Swedish parts of Minnesota for Scandinavian tourists and business people. She has two daughters, Elise and Kristin. "Kristin is interested in baking. It will be interesting to see if they carry on the traditions some day."

Ann grinds the potatoes in a manual meat grinder, on a coarse setting. If a food processor is used, the potatoes are too finely ground, she has found. Ann serves the sausage with yellow mustard; others prefer to accompany it with lingonberries. And what better accompaniment for Swedish potato sausage than more potatoes. Serve the potatoes boiled; no French fries allowed!

Marci and Ann make Swede sausage for family and friends only at Christmastime, while Dave Carlson is a real pro. He's one of the owners—along with his brother Dale, John Shimshock and Dave Anderson—of Ready Meats on Johnson Street in northeast Minneapolis. Dave Carlson has been making potato sausage for years, as did his dad and uncles before him. There really were men named Ready in the business at one time. "My Uncle Arnie and the Readys had the original business and my dad, Cliff, and George Shimshock joined after the war." In addition to the potato sausage, the meat market also sells *lutfisk*, pickled herring, *sylta*, and many, many packages of Swedish meatball mix.

There are many different recipes for Swedish potato sausage. Dave said there must be thousands of different recipes. "People come in here all the time and ask us to taste their sausage. Then they tell us we should be selling it." Christmas, of course, is the big sausage season

Dave Carlson, one of the owners of Ready Meats, is shown behind the counter of the meat market. Photo courtesy of Dave Carlson.

Ready Meats' Potato Sausage

This is the sausage that is so popular with Ready Meats' customers in Minneapolis. The amounts can vary, but the proportions should remain the same.

one-third ground beef
one-third peeled, ground potato
one-third ground pork
one quarter of an onion, chopped, for every 10-pound batch of sausage.
beef casings, cut to desired size and rinsed in cold water

Mix beef, potato and pork together. Spice mildly with salt, pepper and a little allspice. Put into sausage casings through a meat grinder, or an inverted angel food pan. Cook as in recipe for *Värmlands Potatiskorv*.

for Ready Meats, which sells two thousand pounds—that's a whole ton—of sausage in the week before Christmas. "We sell about a hundred pounds of it in a normal week," said Dave. Recipes for the sausage may call for pork alone, or a combination of pork with beef or veal, and different spices.

Making any sausage is a slippery proposition, as the beef casings are tough and slimy to work with. Some people might even say, "Oh, ish!" Beef casings for the sausage can be purchased at Ready Meats and at Ingebretsen Scandinavian Foods in Minneapolis, as well as at other meat markets and supermarkets. Whole allspice can be found in the spice section of some large grocery stores.

Marci Osborne's Potato Sausage

Marci Elfstrom Osborne uses her mother's recipe for potato sausage, which calls for more potato than the other two recipes given here.

3 lb. ground beef
2 lb. ground pork
10 lb. white potatoes, peeled and coarsely ground
2 Marci-sized (that means small!) handfuls of salt
enough pepper (until it looks good, Marci says)
Add the amount of cinnamon, allspice and ground
    ginger that can be balanced (separately) on the
    end of a teaspoon handle
beef casings, cut to size and rinsed in cold water.

Mix all ingredients together and stuff beef casings. Makes 15 to 20 rings of sausage. Marci turns the ends of the casings in, rather than tying them. Simmer until the potato is done.

Värmlands Potatiskorv

(Värmland's potato sausage)

This recipe was handed down to Ann-Christine Moonen from her mother.

8 or 9 medium potatoes, peeled and ground or
    chopped to the size of a pea
40 to 45 whole allspice, crushed
1 medium onion, finely chopped
1 tbsp. salt
1½ lb. ground pork
½ lb. beef casing, rinsed inside and out with cold
    water and cut into desired lengths
cotton string

Mix potatoes, allspice, onion, salt and pork together in a large bowl. Tie one end of each length of casing with string. Hold the open end of the casing around the spout of a meat grinder or around the center spout of an inverted angel food cake pan with one hand. With the other hand, feed the sausage mixture into the casing, pushing it down to the bottom as you go and easing any air bubbles out the top. Leave about one inch of casing free of sausage to let the sausage expand as it cooks and tie off with string again. Prick each sausage, place in a pan with enough water to cover and bring to a boil. Reduce heat to a simmer for about 45 minutes to an hour, testing to make sure the potato is fully cooked. This can be frozen after it cools.

Ingebretsen's
Need we say more?

Every December, my mother would say, "I feel a trip to Ingebretsen's coming on." She wasn't the only one to get a sudden craving for some good solid sausage and a couple of pounds of meatball mix for Christmas Eve. When we drove over from north Minneapolis to Ingebretsen's on the south side, it seemed like half of Minneapolis had the same idea. We were never there when the line extended out the door and down the block, but I know it has. "It's a tradition for some people to come and stand in line at Christmas. They meet their friends here," said Julie Ingebretsen, manager of the gift shop. Christmas is "the season" for Ingebretsen's. "I don't do anything else during November and December. I work about 75 hours during the week then." The crowds are heaviest in the two weeks before Christmas.

But back to my mom and me: after we were done with the sausage and meatball buying, we'd usually buy a stingy quarter-pound of lamb roll (hey, that stuff is expensive!). We'd eat it at home in secret, without offering it to the rest of the family, as a reward for battling our way through the Christmas crowd in front of the vast meat counter.

Ingebretsen's was still called the Model Market—as its former owner called it—when this photo was taken in the 1930s. The store still sells lingonberries, salt fish, Norwegian (and Swedish) cheese and many imported canned goods. Photo courtesy of Ingebretsen's.

Ingebretsen's founder, Charles Ingebretsen, who was a Norwegian immigrant, is at left at the meat counter. The store has remained at its current location—1601 East Lake Street in Minneapolis—since 1921. Photo courtesy of Ingebretsen's.

Ingebretsen's isn't just a meat market or a gift shop; it's an island of Nordicity (yup, I did make that word up), a legendary outpost of Scandinavian cuisine, crafts and culture. "It's old-fashioned in a lot of ways. Most people who work here are pretty much Scandinavian. People come in for the ambiance. It's sort of a Scandinavian-American community center and information center," said Julie.

Julie had a vision of what running a gift shop would be like when she took over the management of Ingebretsen's gift shop in south Minneapolis in 1974.

"I was sort of in between jobs—I had decided that teaching wasn't what I wanted to do. My dad (Charles "Bud" Ingebretsen, son of the founder, also named Charles) and his partner asked me if I wanted to run the gift shop. "I remember having this picture in my mind of buying some stuff, putting it on a shelf, sitting by the cash register and being able to read a lot." She laughs when she thinks how naïve she was.

The shop has expanded a couple of times since Julie started managing it. Her dad and Warren Dahl (both Norwegians) are still partners, but the day-to-day running of the gift shop and needlework portions of the complex is Julie's job and Steve Dahl runs the meat market. The shop has been on Bloomington and Lake since 1921, when it called itself The Model Market.

Even before 1921, Norwegian immigrant Charles Ingebretsen had a shop on Seven Corners for a few years. At the time he moved to Bloomington and Lake, there were two other butcher shops on the block. Still, business was brisk in the days before modern refrigeration. "We were on the streetcar line and people would come in every day to buy meat for supper," said Julie.

At first, Ingebretsen's was just another meat market,

Julie Ingebretsen manages the gift shop and is active in Bloomington-Lake neighborhood groups. Photo courtesy of Ingebretsen's.

not a specialist in Scandinavian foods. "My grandfather said when they came here, they were going to be American," said Julie, echoing the statement made by so many Scandinavian immigrants through the years. That philosophy changed with the times and Julie's dad and Warren gradually saw the wisdom of catering to the Scandinavian market.

Now they come by the carload to stock up on Swedish sausage and other Scandinavian delicacies and to browse and buy examples of beautiful contemporary Nordic crafts as well as the more standard gift shop items. Ingebretsen's and the American Swedish Institute's Museum Shop are now the only Scandinavian gift shops in Minneapolis and Julie is continually making an effort to introduce quality Scandinavian crafts to customers. "We like to promote the traditional skills, things that are handmade by small-scale artisans. We went to a trade show to do buying, but I'd like to go into the countryside and find things." With many of the traditional items, such as the handsome wrought iron work and the birchbark containers that Ingebretsen's carries, it is an old skill with a new twist. "The skill is the same, but the design changes," Julie explained. "I like introducing people to a cultural path, helping them to get a feel for that culture." Ingebretsen's has a website and a catalog, too, and a lot of business now comes through the catalog.

For a while, the neighborhood around Ingebretsen's got pretty rough, and a decision had to be made about whether to chicken out and follow many of the customers out of the inner city. But Ingebretsen's stayed and Julie has taken a very active role in the neighborhood association. "I like that very much," she said. After the decision was made, Julie expanded the store, devoting a new shop, just a door down the block, to needlework supplies, lessons in needle arts—including knitting, tatting and Hardanger work—and a tempting supply of clothes from Norway and Sweden. In addition to the classes, Ingebretsen's sponsors visits by crafts people and authors.

Now here's the funny part: Julie didn't really get interested in her heritage until she took over the gift shop. Although the family had torsk (note: not *lutefisk*) for Christmas Eve, Julie said, "I was raised an Irish Catholic." Her mom was Irish and Julie went to Catholic schools. If that isn't a perfect description of the melting pot I don't know what is.

Speaking of Irish, we should say that Mike Svendahl, a Norwegian who's been behind the meat counter at

Ingebretsen's Dala-style mural, by Judy Nelson Kjenstad, depicts a Midsommar celebration. Photo courtesy of Ingebretsen's

Ingebretsen's for 36 years, said that one of the guys responsible for the potato sausage is an Irishman, Gary Coleman. Mike, whose dad was from Norway, said a lot of the items requested, especially at Christmas and Easter are the "farm foods" of Scandinavia, including *julskinka* (an unsmoked Christmas ham), yellow dried peas, *Västerbotten* cheese, two kinds of *sylta* (head cheese), blood sausage, pickled herring and on and on. "Especially around the holidays, people come in here and buy stuff because it reminds them of home," said. Mike. The real Swedes don't come for the *lutfisk* or potato sausage so much, said Mike. "Those are more Minnesota Swede things."

The American Swedish Institute
Swedish culture and coffee, too

The American Swedish Institute is the epicenter of Swedish and Swedish-American culture, certainly for the Twin Cities, and perhaps for all of North America. The castle-like structure at 2600 Park Avenue in south Minneapolis, means different things to different people. It's a haven for homesick Swedes, who come to the Twin Cities for business reasons or to spend a year or two working for a family or because they are married to Americans. At the Institute, they can have a cup of coffee, get a whiff of meatballs or other Swedish soul food cooking in the kitchen, read the Swedish newspapers in the lounge and find someone to *prata på svenska* (chat in Swedish).

The ASI gets its share of visiting Swedes, too, who come—not to link with Sweden—but to discover Swedish America. Tour groups from Sweden show up regularly at the 33-room house. After seeing the Institute and other sights in the Twin Cities, the Swedes usually make a beeline for Lindstrom and Scandia, looking for signs of the early Swedish settlements there and eager to trace the path of the fictional Karl Oskar and Kristina, the Swedish immigrants brought vividly to life in Vilhelm Moberg's novels and in the later films.

Swedes aren't the only ones coming to look the ASI over. Church groups, school kids, and many affinity groups—even the Antique Doorknob Collectors of America (really)—come to look at the beautiful house. Public tours are held three times a week, with additional tours on request. Individual visitors are welcome to look around and volunteers are always around to answer questions even when a tour is not scheduled.

Tours begin in the magnificent Grand Hall, dominated by a two-story fireplace, its mantel and the figures that flank it carved from rich, brownish-red African mahogany. Off the Grand Hall is the Dining Room, which has more carving than any other room in the house—and that is saying something.

Centerpiece of the Grand Hall in the American Swedish Institute in Minneapolis is a magnificent, two-story fireplace, carved of African mahogany. Photo courtesy of the American Swedish Institute.

The American Swedish Institute, at 2600 Park Avenue in Minneapolis, is castle-like in appearance. Photo courtesy of the American Swedish Institute.

The Music Room, also on the first floor, represents a one-man marathon of cherub-carving. Around the room and on the fireplace, master woodcarver Ulrich Steiner created 52 winged cherubs of Honduran mahogany. According to one of Steiner's descendants, the carver reportedly said he hoped he would never have to carve another cherub in his life after he finished the 52nd.[1]

On the way up to the second floor, visitors stop and take in the Visby Window, a glowing stained glass creation that is a copy of a painting in the National Museum in Stockholm, Sweden. On the second floor is the library that belonged to Swan J. Turnblad, the Swedish-American newspaper publisher who had the house built early in the twentieth century. The other major second-floor rooms, once bedrooms for the Turnblad family, are now used for exhibits, both permanent and temporary. On the third floor, in the Ballroom, is a permanent exhibit depicting Swedish-American life in Minneapolis and St. Paul. Interactive stations let visitors hear the music of an earlier day as well as see for themselves what immigrant residents of the area wore, what they did and how they lived.

The Institute also functions as a museum and exhibit gallery. Only a portion of the collection is displayed, however, as even 33 rooms aren't enough space for the massive collection of furniture, glass, books, textiles and other artifacts. On the second floor, one room has a permanent display of Swedish glass—colored and clear, modern and traditional, funky and formal—made by Sweden's master glass artists.

In an adjacent room is a display of wood carvings, a traditional Swedish art that came to the United States with the immigrants. Also on that floor is an exhibit of memorabilia from the Turnblad family and from

There are 11 porcelain stoves (kakelugnar) in the American Swedish Institute building at 2600 Park Avenue in Minneapolis. This one, in the second-story library, is deep green. Photo courtesy of the American Swedish Institute.

Svenska Amerikanska Posten, the newspaper that Swan J. Turnblad published.

The American Swedish Institute also has many other roles to play: it is a teacher, transmitting the Swedish

Prins Bertils Bullar

(cardamom sweet rolls)

The late Prince Bertil of Sweden visited the American Swedish Institute on several occasions. For his visits, and for other visitors over the years, many volunteers, including Jenny Johnson, who emigrated from Sweden when she was 21 years old, have baked countless rolls and cookies. The Prince ate Jenny's cardamom sweet rolls on one visit and liked them very much. The next time he came, Jenny had a batch specially baked for him. She even gave him a box of the rolls to take with him. Since then, the folks at the Institute have called them *Prins Bertils Bullar* (Prince Bertil's rolls). This recipe makes 80 rolls, so invite a lot of people over for coffee after you make them. They freeze well, too.

As for Jenny, she is 95 years old and still going strong. She was a seamstress and made her last wedding dress, for her grandson's bride, when she was 90 years old. Jenny's own bridal gown was a beautiful lace creation that she made herself. Her rolls are just as exquisite as her sewing!

6 tsp. yeast
¼ c. warm water
1 tbsp. sugar
1 qt. whole milk
⅓ lb. butter (one and one-third sticks)
⅓ lb. margarine (one and one-third sticks)
2 c. sugar
4 egg yolks, plus 1 whole egg
3–4 tsp. freshly ground cardamom

approximately 12 c. white flour
⅓ c. butter, softened, to spread on the dough
one egg, plus one egg white, lightly whipped, to brush on rolls
pearl sugar and chopped nuts, if desired, to sprinkle on rolls

Combine yeast, warm water and 1 tablespoon sugar in a small bowl and let stand until foamy. Meanwhile, warm the milk in a large saucepan until lukewarm. Add butter and margarine and let melt. Do not let butter brown. In a large bowl or mixer bowl, combine eggs and sugar and mix or stir until foamy. Add the butter and milk mixture, cardamom, a little flour and the yeast mixture. Slowly add flour, a little at a time, until you have added about 10 cups. The rest of the flour is used when rolling out the dough. Knead on a floured board. If you have used a mixer, knead only a little. If you are making the rolls by hand, knead a bit more. Place in a large (or even two) bowls and let rise, covered, until doubled. Divide dough in three parts, for easier handling. Roll out on a well-floured board (this is a soft dough) until the dough is about one-third inch thick and about 12 inches wide. Spread softened butter along one half, horizontally. Sprinkle a little sugar over the butter, then fold over to make a six-inch wide piece of dough. Cut strips about three-quarter inch wide and six inches long. Score a line down the center of each strip—purely for decorative purposes. Twist dough strips and tuck ends under to form rolls. Repeat with remaining two portions of dough. Place rolls on lightly greased baking sheets and let rise until nearly doubled. Brush tops with the egg and egg white mixture and sprinkle with pearl sugar and nuts, if desired. Bake at 350 10 to 12 minutes.

language, traditions and culture to students of all ages and backgrounds via classes open to all; it is an entertainer, offering concerts, dance performances, plays and many other special events to the public; it is a pathway to the past, helping families discover information about their forebears; it is a link with modern Sweden, bringing officials, celebrities and scholars to the Twin Cities; and, for many of us, it is the nearest thing to hog heaven, with its monthly *smörgåsbord* that nearly keeps real noshers satisfied until the next month's.

The Institute has hosted kings and presidents in its time; the coffee was on for them and it will be on for you, too.

This may have been taken for Swan Turnblad's confirmation at Vasa Lutheran Church in 1876. Photo courtesy of the American Swedish Institute.

Swan J. Turnblad
A son of Småland makes it big

Swan J. Turnblad, who built the house that later became the American Swedish Institute, has been dead nearly seventy years, but visitors to the house at 2600 Park Avenue are still curious about the man and his life.

Swan and his family, like most Swedish immigrants, probably came to America because times were so tough. The late 1860s were the peak years for emigration from Sweden, with Swedes leaving in droves in 1868 and 1869.

Snow blanketed the American Swedish Institute when this picture was taken. The gate has since been replaced by a larger one. Photo courtesy of the American Swedish Institute.

From 1845 to 1930, about 1.25 million Swedes—nearly a quarter of the population—left Sweden for North America. Only in Ireland, Norway and Iceland did a larger percentage of the population emigrate.[2]

Swan was born on Oct. 7, 1860, in Småland, in southern Sweden. He and his family left Sweden in 1868, shortly before Swan's 8th birthday, and eventually joined Swan's half-brother, who had emigrated earlier, in Vasa, Minnesota. Vasa, founded by Swedish immigrants, was very much a Swedish community then. Swan lived there until he moved to Minneapolis, when he was probably in his late teens. In the *Minneapolis City Directory* of 1881–1883 he is listed living with his sister and brother-in-law at 127 Cedar Avenue in Minneapolis and working as a compositor for the *Minnesota stats tidning*.[3]

Publisher Swan Turnblad is seated at his desk in the office of Svenska Amerikanska Posten. *The newspaper once had the largest circulation of any Swedish language newspaper in the United States. Photo courtesy of the American Swedish Institute.*

At the time Swan started working as a compositor, Swedish-language newspapers were common. When the newspaper that Swan was associated with for most of his career, *Svenska Amerikanska Posten,* began publishing in 1885, four other weekly Swedish-language papers were published in Minnesota—*Skaffaren och Minnesota stats tidning, Svenska Folkets Tidning, Svenska Kristna Härolden* and *Mission-Bladet.*[4]

Svenska Amerikanska Posten began as a temperance advocate. In the first issue, the paper proclaimed that it was "An Independent Swedish Political Newspaper Devoted to the promotion of Temperance, Good Morals and the elevation of Society."[5] Over the years, there was less emphasis on temperance. Swan went to work for *Posten* first as a typesetter, was a stockholder in 1885 and is listed as manager of the paper in the 1886 Dual City Business Directory.[6] Gradually, *SAP* increased its circulation—due to Turnblad's innovations, such as early use of color, national advertising and smart marketing—and eventually reached a circulation high of more than 50,000 according to Ulf Jonas Björk, a journalism professor and author.

Although we tend to consider Swan a Swede first, his success may have been more of an American phenomenon. Author Ulf Jonas Björk quotes Chicago journalist C.F. Peterson, who wrote that Swan was "more American than Swedish, i.e., bolder and more energetic in his way of doing business, calmer and more calculating . . . which made him a 'great success as a businessman.'"[7]

Swan had married Christina Nilsson, another Swedish immigrant, in 1883 and their only child, Lillian, was born in 1884. The Turnblads grew wealthy. They went on trips to Europe, something average Scandinavian immigrants could never dream of. They built a thirty-three

The house on Park Avenue, which took several years to build, was completed in 1908. Although the Turnblads may have lived in it at times, they were listed as living at 500 South 7th Street in Minneapolis in the 1922 Minneapolis City Directory.[9] Christina Turnblad died in 1929. In December of that year, Swan turned the house and the newspaper over to the newly established American Institute of Swedish Arts, Literature, and Science, now known as the American Swedish Institute.[10] Swan and his daughter, who never married, lived across the street from the Turnblad house, at 2615 Park Avenue, in apartments until Swan died in 1933. Lillian Turnblad continued as publisher of *SAP* until it was sold to Chicago's *Svenska Amerikanaren Tribunen* in 1940.

Swan and Christina Turnblad and their only child, Lillian, are shown in this photo, taken circa 1889. Photo courtesy of the American Swedish Institute.

Swan Turnblad was the first person in Minneapolis to own a commercially manufactured automobile. He bought the 1899 Waverley Electric in 1900 for $1,250. Photo courtesy of the American Swedish Institute.

room house on Park Avenue, where the elite of Minneapolis lived, and they also battled lawsuits stemming from the charge that Swan undervalued *SAP* stock in 1885, leading many stockholders to sell their stock to him at a lower price. A suit brought in 1908 by former stockholders was at first decided in Swan's favor and later overturned by the Minnesota Supreme Court.[8]

Bruce Karstadt is executive director of the American Swedish Institute. Peterson Portraits, courtesy of the American Swedish Institute.

Bruce Karstadt
On the state of Swedishness

Bruce Karstadt came to Minneapolis as the director of the American Swedish Institute a decade ago from that other hotbed of Swedish-American culture, Lindsborg, Kansas. In his ten years as director, he's seen the ASI grow greatly in membership and reach out to other cultures, rather than maintaining a de-facto 'Swedes only' policy.

Bruce is a big bear of a guy, a warm-hearted philosopher with a historian's high regard for the past and a practical eye for the future. He came to the director's job after working first as a lawyer and later as an administrator at Bethany College in Lindsborg. At Bethany, he helped organize all the touring cultural groups, exhibits, films, concerts, etc., that came from Sweden as part of the year-long national celebration called 'New Sweden '88.' "That was very meaningful work and it brought me in contact with official Sweden and people in Sweden for the first time," said Bruce. "It gave me a taste of the relationship between Sweden and the U.S. It was different from what I had experienced growing up as part of a Swedish-American community."

The New Sweden assignment pointed him in a new direction. "I've always been interested in history and family history [his mother's grandparents all came from Sweden], but I never had put it into context that it could be done for a living. When the job as director opened up here, friends here encouraged me to apply." Another factor, he added with a grin, was that "Ingrid Bergman made a reference to the American Swedish Institute in 'Murder on the Orient Express.'"

He didn't find the glamorous Swedish movie star here, but he's been happy and challenged just the same. Asked whether the state of Swedishness in the Twin Cities has changed over the years, he responded thoughtfully. "The feelings that people have about Sweden are the same as they always were. There is still a desire to celebrate that heritage both in the home and in public. We live in history, and history lives in us. But there is a difference now because we have more opportunity to bring people from Sweden here to let us know about the Sweden of today."

"I would say the state of Swedishness here is really quite good, but it is changing. Some of the older clubs and lodges are facing challenging times, but new clubs are always being formed. There is a constant rebirth of the Swedish experience. The Nordic Roots music festival is a good example of that. It draws many people from the younger generation who may or may not connect it with Scandinavia."

This renaissance of interest in Swedish culture takes many forms, Bruce added. "You find it in interest in the new cuisine of Sweden, in films, music, literature and the language. You find it in the interest people take in the Swedish approach to the environment, to peace, to conflict resolution, to the Nobel prizes and to design and sports."

"People here are redefining what Sweden is for them. Here at the American Swedish Institute we must respect the past, but build for tomorrow. There is room for both the past and the future and we have to approach both from a multi-generational perspective. We are now also trying to develop an audience that values the Swedish-American experience from a cross-cultural perspective. We know, based on our own immigrant history, that we have a lot to offer to people interested in contemporary immigration issues. We have extraordinary resources here for anyone interested in the challenges of modern immigration here and also in Sweden.

The Swedish experience takes some unusual turns, Bruce said. "There is nothing more surprising to our perception of Swedishness, for instance, than to find that some of the Somali taxi drivers here in Minneapolis speak perfect Swedish because they have spent several years in Sweden before immigrating here."

The Institute has broadened its focus over the years, he added. "We have to continue removing any barriers to the integration of our members with the community. We need to provide the kinds of programs that reach out to as many people as possible and at the same time to make sure that our collection reflects our history."

There are many different ways for Swedish-Americans to proclaim their heritage, Bruce said. "We have to respect how different people express their Swedishness and help them do that, if we can. Some people wear a folk costume, some people love to come to the *smörgåsbord* here and some people like to put a bumper sticker on their car that identifies them as Swedish."

Perhaps the most unusual way one man cherished his heritage was through a tattoo. "We got a request from a proud Swedish-American who was in prison in another state. He wanted a line drawing of the Institute to use as a pattern. He was going to have it tattooed on his back, under the two Valkyrie-like women on flying horses that he already had tattooed. Now this guy was expressing his Swedishness in that way, whatever judgment you would make of it. So I said, He's going to do it anyway, so let's send him a decent line drawing, and we did."

Here are old friends from our Camden neighborhood at a reunion in August. The author is kneeling in front, next to Steve Leverentz. Shirley Shaft is at right. Second row, from left, are Russ Nieland, Jim Gillespie, Lauri Elfstrom Bassett, Larry Elfstrom, Ginny Elfstrom (partly obscured), Marci Elfstrom Osborne, Jim Shaft, Jim Fairweather, Jimmy Shaft. Back row, Brian and Barb Storm, Austin Gillespie, Pixie Elfstrom Haug, Joe Gillespie, Dave Leverentz, Mike Gillespie, and Tom and Winnie Collins. Photo courtesy of Austin Gillespie and Jackie Gillespie.

Epilogue

Well, now this book is written and I am sorry to see it end. During the course of researching and writing it, I had a wonderful time making new friends and getting reacquainted with old friends and old haunts. Several of the people profiled in the book were among the last immigrants to come to the United States before the great wave of immigration subsided. They are old now and leaving us all too quickly, but their memories of their early days were largely fresh in their minds as we talked. They were happy to tell me their stories and I was pleased to hear them and write them down. Along the way, I realized that what I was doing was making a historical record, for history is not just wars and the dips in the economy, after all. History is also Gunhild Anderson learning English in night school after she put in a full day working as a maid and Axel Ohman laying brick but still having time to organize a Swedish-American Athletic Association and it is a little girl promising to marry the tall Swede who helped her down from a tree.

My own history surfaced, too. An unexpected pleasure was that writing the book brought me back in touch with my own past. Several times during the last year I drove across the bridge over the Mississippi River on my way back to my old neighborhood in Camden, at the city's northern end, looking for my own childhood as much as trolling for Swedes. Driving around, thinking about my neighborhood, I slowly began to realize that all my life—particularly when I was young—I have been a part of a community so suffused with echoes of Sweden and Norway—muted though they may have been—that it seemed the norm. It was a wonderful time and a wonderful place to grow up.

Fittingly, many of my old neighbors got together in Camden Park for a reunion in mid-August, just as I was finishing the book. It was fantastic weather, the food was great and of course none of us had changed a bit! It was a wonderful way to end my search for stories from the Swedish Twin Cities. Our own stories—though we had all heard them before—still sounded sweet and funny. Yes—there really is no place like home.

Not for Swedes Only

Some festivals and events in the Twin Cities

This is a partial listing of the Swedish-oriented festivals and events in Minneapolis and St. Paul. All except the morning Lucia Day program are open to the public. Please watch the newspapers for more complete information.

Smörgåsbords are offered monthly from September through May at the American Swedish Institute (ASI). Advance reservations are necessary. The ASI is located at 2600 Park Avenue South in Minneapolis. Call 612-871-4907 for more information, including prices.

January

Until the second Sunday in January, five rooms at the American Swedish Institute remain decorated in the Christmas style of each of the five countries of the Nordic region—Sweden, Norway, Denmark, Sweden and Iceland. See ASI details above. There is an admission charge at the Institute.

June

Midsommar Dag (Midsummer Day) celebration is generally held on the third Saturday in June at the American Swedish Institute. Events include raising the maypole and dancing around it. Free admission. See ASI details above.

Svenskarnas Dag (Swedes' Day) is held on the fourth Sunday in June in Minnehaha Park in south Minneapolis. The day includes speeches, and folk dancing. Many families plan picnics in conjunction with the events. Free.

September–January

This is prime *lutfisk*-and-meatball dinner season. It goes into high gear in late September. Many people go church-supper hopping all across the Twin Cities and suburbs to get their *lutfisk* fix. Two of the big ones are noted below. Some require tickets in advance and some are sure sell-outs, so act fast. Notices are often in community newspapers as well as church bulletins and newsletters.

November

The American Swedish Institute holds its Christmas Fairs on the first and third Saturdays in November. Christmas ornaments and other items from Sweden are for sale and Swedish-style refreshments are available. Admission is charged. See ASI details above.

From the day after Thanksgiving until after Christmas, the American Swedish Institute annually displays five of its rooms decorated in accordance with the Christmas style of each of the five Nordic countries—Sweden, Norway, Denmark, Iceland and Finland. Each room has a table set to reflect a different country. Admission is charged. See ASI details above.

December

Mount Olivet Lutheran Church's annual *lutfisk* dinner—first come, first served—is usually the first Friday of December. The church is at 5025 Knox Avenue South in Minneapolis. Call 612-929-7651 for information.

The annual *lutfisk* dinner at the ASI is held on the first Sunday in December. Call for information on tickets, which go on sale at least a month in advance. ASI details are above.

Lucia Day programs are held at the ASI on December 13th, which is Lucia Day. The morning program is for members only. At least one other program is held on the same day or sometimes on a weekend day. Tickets go quickly; call early for them. See ASI details above.

Julotta, the early Christmas service is Swedish, is held at Augustana Lutheran Church, in downtown Minneapolis, early on Christmas morning. The church is at 11th Avenue South and Seventh Street. The phone number is 612-332-8595.

Endnotes

Chapter One—Just Another Swede Town

Just another Swede town

1. John Rice, "The Swedes," in *They Chose Minnesota—A Survey of the State's Ethnic Groups*, edited by June Drenning Holmquist (St. Paul: Minnesota Historical Society Press, 1981) p. 264.

Chapter Two—So Far Away in the World

Introduction

1. Letter from Nils Gustavsson in Varberg, Sweden, to Bror Heurbeck in St. Paul, Minnesota, dated March 21, 1954. A copy of the letter, in Swedish, is in the archives of the American Swedish Institute, Minneapolis, Minnesota.

Bertha Brunius—A light heart on the frontier

2. Letter from Bertha Brunius in St. Anthony, Minnesota, to unknown persons in Sweden, dated March 26, 1856. A copy of the English translation of the letter, done by an unknown person, is in the archives of the American Swedish Institute.

3. "Death of Mrs. J. O. Brunius," *Chaska Herald*, June 20, 1895.

4. Lucie K. Hartley, *The Carver Story*, (Lucie K. Hartley, 1993), p. 127.

5. Letter from Prof. Teddy Brunius to Anne Gillespie Lewis, January 20, 2001.

6. Prof. Teddy Brunius, "Swedish Settler Writes Home—Life at Carver, Minn., a Century Ago," *American Swedish Institute Bulletin*, Vol. 12, No. 1, Summer, 1957, pp. 12–13.

Albin E. Johnson—An Immigrant's Paper Trail

7. All documents referred to are in the archives of the American Swedish Institute, Minneapolis, Minnesota.

8. Robert Owen, *"I dag skulle jag ha stannat,"* *Smålandsposten,* July 19, 1976, p. 11. Reprinted with permission of the *Smålandsposten* and Robert Owen.

John P. Wallberg—Next Christmas I'll be home

9. The original letters are in the possession of John Wallberg's daughter, Lorraine Wallberg McGrath. Copies are in the archives of the American Swedish Institute.

Chapter Three—The New Newcomers

Introduction

1. Rice, p. 254.

Chapter Four—Swedes at Work

Introduction

1. The Rev. Marion Daniel Shutter, ed., *History of Minneapolis: Gateway to the Northwest,* 3 volumes (Chicago-Minneapolis: S.J. Clarke Publishing Co., 1923) Vol. I, pp. 669–670.

Annie Robertson—"All rests with Annie the cook"

2. Jenny Olstad Haroldsen, interviewed February 15, 1975, by her daughter, Ruth Haroldsen (no other last name recorded) and son Kenneth Haroldsen, and transcribed by Lynne McCarthy, August 1, 1989. Side II (215–280), Minnesota Historical Society, St. Paul, Minnesota.

3. Carlotte Wickstrom Carlson, no date, interviewed by Evelyn Olson and Edna Reasoner, Minnesota Historical Society, St. Paul, Minnesota.

4. Personal communication from Eileen DeWald to the author, August 3, 2001.

5. The Alexander Ramsey Papers and Records, Minnesota Historical Society, St. Paul, Minnesota, Microfilm Roll 44, Frame 1249.

6. U.S. Census of 1880, roll 630, frame 363, p. 18, sup. 3, En. 8, No. 22, 101–109. Copy in the Minnesota Historical Society's History Center, St. Paul, Minnesota.

7. The Alexander Ramsey Papers and Records, Minnesota Historical Society, St. Paul, Minnesota, Microfilm Roll 31, Frame 87.

8. Ibid., Roll 31, Frame 174.

9. Ibid., Roll, 31, Frame 584.

10. Ibid., Roll 46, Frame 859.

11. Ibid., Roll 46, Frame 860.

12. Ibid., Roll 30, Frame 42.

13. Ibid., Roll 30, Frame 53.

14. Ibid., Roll 32, Frame 713.

15. Ibid., Roll 32, Frame 199.

16. Ibid., Roll 31, Frame 204.

17. Ibid., Roll 35, Frame 19.

18. Ibid., Roll 32, Frame 569.

19. Ibid., Roll 35, Frame 302–303.

20. Document regarding Anna Robertson's estate, filed in Probate Court in Ramsey County in the State of Minnesota, November 29, 1927.

21. Petition for administration of Anna Robertson's estate, filed in St. Paul, in Ramsey County, in the State of Minnesota, on April 21, 1926.

22. "Domestic in home of Ramsey is dead," *St. Paul Pioneer Press*, April 20, 1926, p. 5.

Annie the cook, Lizzie the nursemaid and thousands of others

23. Jenny Walen, in an oral interview, October 11, 1991, Minneapolis Historical Society, St. Paul, Minnesota.

24. *Biennial report of the Bureau of Labor Statistics of the State of Minnesota for the two years ending 1887–1888.* [Minnesota]: Printed by the authority of the Legislature, 1888– ([Minnesota]: Thos. A. Clark & Co.). A copy is in the Minnesota Historical Center Library, St. Paul, Minnesota.

25. Ibid, p. 147.

26. Ibid., p. 150.

27. Ibid., p. 151.

28. Ibid.

29. Ibid., p. 152.

30. Ibid., p. 153.

31. Ibid.

32. Ibid., p. 154.

33. Ibid., p. 155.

34. Ibid., pp. 157–158.

35. Ibid., pp. 160–161.

36. Ibid., p. 161.

37. Ibid.

Chapter Five—Swedes at Play

1. Stew Thornley, *Basketball's Original Dynasty/The History of the Lakers.* (Minneapolis: Nodin Press, 1989), p. 17.

2. Thornley, p. 18.

3. Ibid., p. 108.

4. Ibid., p. 101.

Chapter Six—Body and Soul

Audrey Grann Johnson—Swedes in stripes

1. Pat Gaarder and Tracey Baker, *From Stripes to Whites, A History of the Swedish Hospital School of Nursing 1899–1973*, (the Swedish Hospital Alumnae Association: 1980), p. ix.

2. Ibid., p. 2.

A Church-going people

3. Book commemorating the 125th Anniversary of First Lutheran Church of St. Paul, Minnesota, 1854–1979, p.10.

4. Ibid., p. 11.

5. Ibid.

6. Ibid., p. 12.

7. Ibid., p. 13.

8. Ibid., p. 14.

9. Ibid., p. 18.

Eric Norelius—A young man and a blind horse

10. Emeroy Johnson, *Eric Norelius/Pioneer Midwest Pastor and Churchman*, copyright © 1954 Augustana Book Concern, admin. Augsburg Fortress. Used by permission, p. 24.

11. Eric Norelius, translated by Emeroy Johnson, *Early Life of Eric Norelius*, copyright © 1934 Augustana Book Concern, admin. Augsburg Fortress. Used by permission, p. 290.

12. Ibid., p. 231–232.

13. Ibid., pp. 286–287.

14. Ibid., pp. 317–319.

Ten little Youngdahls and how they grew

15. Robert Esbjornson, *A Christian in Politics: Luther W. Youngdahl*, (Minneapolis: T. S. Denison & Company, 1955). Esbjornson's book provides a close look at Luther Youngdahl and his family. The chapter titled "Sons and Brothers," pp. 65–78, has many references to the family's activities.

16. Kay Miller, "Ruth Youngdahl Nelson," *Minneapolis Tribune Picture* magazine, November 7, 1982, pp. 4–12.

17. Esbjornson, p. 258.

18. Ibid., p. 260.

Chapter Seven—The Next Generations

Wendell Anderson— From the east side to the king's side

1. Committee for the Inauguration of Wendell R. Anderson, *Governors of Minnesota 1849–1971* (St. Paul, 1971).

Chapter Eight—For a Swedish Accent

The American Swedish Institute— Swedish coffee and culture, too

1. Anne Gillespie Lewis, *The American Swedish Institute: Turnblad's Castle* (Minneapolis: The American Swedish Institute, 1999) p. 52.

Swan J. Turnblad—A son of Småland makes it big

2. Rice, p. 254.

3. Lawrence G. Hammerstrom, *A Chronology of the Events in the Lives of Swan J. Turnblad*, Christina Nilsson Turnblad, Lillian Zenobia Turnblad. December, 1997.

4. Ulf Jonas Björk, "Proud to be a Yellow Journal: *Svenska Amerikanska Posten*, An Immigrant Newspaper with American Accents," presented at the Swedish Life in the Twin Cities Conference, St. Paul, Minnesota, 1996, p. 3.

5. Hammerstrom, p. 3.

6. Ibid., pp. 2–3.

7. Björk, pp. 5–6.

8. Lewis, pp.37–38.

9. Ibid., p. 54.

10. Nils William Olsson and Lawrence G. Hammerstrom, "Swan Johan Turnblad and the Founding of the American Swedish Institute," presented at the Swedish Life in the Twin Cities Conference, St. Paul, Minnesota, 1996, p. 6.

Bibliography

Alexander Ramsey Papers and Records. Microfilm. (St.Paul: Minnesota Historical Society).

Björk, Ulf Jonas. "Proud to Be a Yellow Journal: *Svenska Amerikanska Posten,* An Immigrant Newspaper with American Accents," presented at the Swedish Life in the Twin Cities Conference, St. Paul, Minnesota, 1996.

Bockelman, Wilfred. *For Such a Time as This.* (Minneapolis: Mount Olivet Lutheran Church, 1994).

Brunius, Bertha. Letter from Bertha Brunius in St. Anthony, Minnesota, to unknown persons in Sweden, dated March 26, 1856. A copy of the English translation of the letter, done by an unknown person, is in the Archives of the American Swedish Institute.

Brunius, Professor Teddy. Letter from Prof. Teddy Brunius to Anne Gillespie Lewis, January 20, 2001.

Brunius, Professor Teddy. "Swedish Settler Writes Home— Life at Carver, Minn., a Century Ago," *American Swedish Institute Bulletin,* Vol. 12, No. 1, Summer, 1957, pp. 12–13.

Carlson, Carlotte Wickstrom. Undated oral history. Interviewed by Evelyn Olson and Edna Reasoner. (St. Paul: Minnesota Historical Society).

Committee for the Inauguration of Wendell R. Anderson, *Governors of Minnesota, 1849–1971.* (St. Paul, 1971).

"Death of Mrs. J. O. Brunius," concerning Bertha Brunius. *Chaska Herald,* June 20, 1895.

Esbjornson, Robert. *A Christian in Politics: Luther W. Youngdahl.* (Minneapolis: T.S. Denison and Company: 1955).

First Biennial Report of the Bureau of Labor Statistics of the State of Minnesota (Thomas A. Clark and Co., 1888).

Gaarder, Pat, and Baker, Tracy. *From Stripes to Whites, A History of the Swedish Hospital School of Nursing 1899–1973.* (Minneapolis: The Swedish Hospital Alumnae Association, 1980).

Grann, Mildred Soderholm. Unpublished diaries kept during studies at the Swedish Hospital School of Nursing, Minneapolis, Minnesota, 1927 to 1930. In the collection of Audrey Grann Johnson.

Gustavsson, Nils. Letter from Nils Gustavsson in Sweden to Bror Heurbeck in St. Paul, Minnesota, dated March 21, 1954. A copy of the letter, in Swedish, is in the Archives of the American Swedish Institute, Minneapolis, Minnesota.

Hammerstrom, Lawrence G. "A Chronology of the Events in the Lives of Swan John Turnblad, Christina Nilsson Turnblad, Lillian Zenobia Turnblad," December, 1997.

Haroldsen, Jenny Olstad. Oral history. Interviewed February 15, 1975, by her daughter, Ruth Haroldsen (no other last name recorded) and son Kenneth Haroldsen, and transcribed by Lynne McCarthy, August 1, 1989. Side II (215–280). (St. Paul: Minnesota Historical Society).

Hartley, Lucie K. *The Carver Story*. (Carver, Minnesot: Lucie K. Hartley, 1993).

History of Minneapolis: Gateway to the Northwest, edited by the Rev. Marion Daniel Shutter. Volume I. (Chicago-Minneapolis: the S.J. Clarke Publishing Co., 1923).

Hoisinton, Daniel J. *A True Nurse, The Story of the Swedish Hospital School of Nursing* (Minneapolis: The Swedish Hospital Alumnae Association, 1999).

Johnson, Albin E. Johnson. Documents regarding education, immigration and U.S. Army service. All documents referred to are in the Albin E. Johnson box in the Archives of the American Swedish Institute, Minneapolis, Minnesota.

Johnson, Emeroy. *Eric Norelius, Pioneer Midwest Pastor and Churchman*. (Rock Island, Illinois: Augustana Book Concern, 1954).

Johnson, Robert R. Memoir of his father, Axel Johnson 1952 (unpublished).

Ledger of the Corona Band (in Swedish), 1921–1926, unpublished ledger of band meetings and expenses.

Lewis, Anne Gillespie. *The American Swedish Institute: Turnblad's Castle*. (Minneapolis: The American Swedish Institute, 1999).

Norelius, Eric. *Early Life of Eric Norelius, 1833–1862,* *a Lutheran Pioneer, his own story rendered into English*. Translation: Emeroy Johnson. (Rock Island, Illinois: Augustana Book Concern, 1934)

Olsson, Nils William, and Hammerstrom, Lawrence G. "Swan Johan Turnblad and the Founding of the American Swedish Institute," presented at the Swedish Life in the Twin Cities Conference, St. Paul, Minnesota, 1996.

125th anniversary of First Lutheran Church (St. Paul, Minnesota: First Lutheran Church, 1979)

Owen, Robert. *"I dag skulle jag ha stannat"* in *Smålandsposten,* July 19, 1976, p. 11. Reprinted with permission of the *Smålandsposten* and Robert Owen.

Rice, John, "The Swedes" in *They Chose Minnesota: A Survey of the State's Ethnic Groups.* Edited by June Drenning Holmquist (St. Paul: Minnesota Historical Society Press, 1981).

Soderholm, Mildred Grann, diaries, 1927–1930 (unpublished).

Thornley, Stew. *Basketball's Original Dynasty: The History of the Lakers,* (Minneapolis: Nodin Press, 1989).

U.S. Census of 1880, roll 630, frame 363, p. 18, sup. 3, En. 8, No. 22, 101–109. Copy in the Minnesota Historical Society's History Center, St. Paul, Minnesota.

Walen, Jenny. Oral history interview. Interviewed October 11, 1991. (St. Paul: Minnesota Historical Society).

Wallberg, John P. The original letters of John Wallberg are in the possession of John Wallberg's daughter, Lorraine Wallberg McGrath. In Swedish. Copies are in the Archives of the American Swedish Institute.

Permissions

Augsburg Fortress, quotes from *Early Life of Eric Norelius* and *Eric Norelius: Pioneer Midwest Pastor and Churchman*.

ICA Förlaget for the recipe for *pinocciotårta*, from *Sju sorters kakor*.

The *St. Paul Pioneer Press*, quote from Annie Robertson's obituary of April 20, 1927.

Wilhelm Hansen A/S, the Swedish lyrics of *Hälsa dem därhemma*.

St. Paul's First Lutheran Church, quotes from the 125th Anniversary Book.

Lucie K. Hartley, quote from *The Carver Story*.

PAN, for the recipe for Rhubarb Cream, from *Vår kokbok* (Rabén & Shogren, 1975).

The American Swedish Institute, for use of material from its Archives and publications.

Professor Teddy Brunius of Uppsala, Sweden, quote from a letter of January 20, 2001 to the author.

The Minnesota Historical Society, quotes from the Alexander Ramsey Papers and Records and from oral histories.

Audrey Grann Johnson, quotes from the unpublished diaries of Mildred Soderholm Grann.

Lorraine Wallberg McGrath, the letters of John Wallberg.

Robert Owen and *Smålandsposten*, quote from an article by Robert Owen in the July 19, 1976 issue of *Smålandsposten*.

The Swedish Hospital Alumnae Association, quotes from *From Stripes to Whites, A History of the Swedish Hospital School of Nursing 1899-1973*.

Cliff Brunzell, quotes from the unpublished ledger of the Corona Band.

Ulf Jonas Björk, references to "Proud to Be a Yellow Journal: *Svenska Amerikanska Posten*, An Immigrant Newspaper with American Accents," presented at the Swedish Life in the Twin Cities Conference, St. Paul, Minnesota, 1996.

Lawrence G. Hammerstrom, references to "A Chronology of the Events in the Lives of Swan John Turnblad, Christina Nilsson Turnblad, Lillian Zenobia Turnblad," December, 1997.

Robert R. Johnson, quotes from his memoir of his father, Axel Johnson.

Recipe Index

Note: All recipes have been tested by the writer

Breads and rolls

Grandma Weberg's Swedish Rye Bread	131
Gunhild's Swedish Rye Bread *(limpa)*	101
Lorraine McGrath's Cardamom Bread	106
Lussekatter (Lucia buns)	141
Prins Bertils Bullar (cardamom sweet rolls)	152

Salads

Sillsallad (herring salad)	142

Main dishes

Audrey Johnson's Lutfisk	116
Kroppkakor (potato dumplings with pork filling)	22
Lorraine's Swedish Meatballs	105
Marci Osborne's Potato Sausage	145
Ready Meats' Potato Sausage	144
Sjömansbiff (sailors' beef)	57
Värmlands Potatiskorv (Värmland's potato sausage)	145

Desserts

Audrey's Rice Ring with Raspberry Sauce	116
Grandmother's Swedish Pancakes	136
Pinocciotårta (meringue torte)	51
Rice Pudding	54
Rhubarb Cream	50

Cookies

Aunt Aggie's Spritz	142
Ginger Snaps	64
Pepparkakor (Ginger Cookies)	142

Coffee

Grace's Egg Coffee	22

Just for fun

Swedish Hot Sauce	116

Index

Alfaby, Fredolf, 104
American Institute of Swedish Arts, Literature and Science, 155
American Swedish Institute, 71, 82, 84, 88, 98–99, 149–157
Andersen, Elmer L., 138
Anderson, Melissa (Lizzie) Caroline Petersen, 65, 66
Anderson & Sandberg Saloon, 80
Anderson, Al, 14–15
Anderson, Ardis Krefting, 15, 23, 24
Anderson, Dave, 144
Anderson, Grace Blomquist, 17, 18–22
Anderson, Gunhild Karlsson, 49, 83, 93–101
Anderson, Hilding, 49, 96–97
Anderson, Jean, 143
Anderson, Jim (Pastor), 125
Anderson, Lois, 18
Anderson, Malcolm Charles (Charlie), 18, 21
Anderson, Natalie, 21
Anderson, Wendell, 136–138
Andersson, Albin, 40
Axel H. Ohman, Inc, 70, 72

Barnes, Alma & Walter, 135
Barnes, Alma Agnes Lund, 134

Bassett, Lauri Elfstrom, 158
Berg, 14, 27
Beyer, Bill, 55–57
Beyer, Emma, 56
Beyer, Kerstin, 56
Beyer, Margareta Jern, 55–57
Bittner, Annette, 98
Bjerk, Evie, 17
Bjerk, Nellie, 17
Björk, Ulf Jonas, 154
Black Gus , 75
Blomquist, Charlie (Carl), 19, 20, 22
Blomquist, Elin & Charles, 17
Blomquist, Grace Audrey Louise (see Anderson), 20–22, 23
Blomquist, the grocer, 14
Blomquist, Vernon, 18
Bockelman, Wilfred, 127
Borlänge, 52
Brakke, Marilyn Pettit, 73
Brosseau, Dawn Carlson, 109
Brunius, Bertha, 33–36
Brunius, Carl Georg, 36
Brunius, Johan Niklas, 36
Brunius, Oswald, 33–36
Brunius, Teddy, 33,36
Brunzell, Cliff, 83–90
Brunzell, Elma Larson, 85
Brunzell, Herbert, 85
Brunzell, Ingrid, 99

Brunzell, Jean, 88
Brynäs Idrottsförening, 102
Bureau of Labor Statistics, State of Minnesota, 67
Burke, Mildred, 134
Butler, Judy, 112

Call of the North, WCCO, 85
Camden, 13, 14, 15, 18–20, 23, 25
Camden Park, 17, 27
Camden Physicians , 17
Camden Theatre , 17
Carlson, Andrew & Mathilda, 108
Carlson, Arne, 138
Carlson, Carlotte Wickstrom, 61
Carlson, Curt, 87, 88
Carlson, Dale, 144
Carlson, Dave, 143–145
Carlson, Don (in Camden) 14
Carlson, Don "Swede," 107
Carlson, Gretchen, 123, 132–133
Carlson, Helene, 107
Carver County, 33
Cathedral of the Pines, 127
Chicago Stags, 108
Coleman, Gary, 148
Collins, Tom and Winnie 158
Compo-Board Factory, 19
Copenhagen (Snuff), 89
Corona Band, 83, 90–93

Dahl, Steve, 147
Dahl, Warren, 143, 147
Dalaförening, 71
Dalarna, Sweden, 32, 52, 69, 71, 93, 129
Dalmålning, 52
Danielson, Oscar, 90
DeWald, Eileen, 61

Ekholm, Anna & Axel, 52
Elfstrom Phyllis (Johnson), 15, 17,
    27–31, 143
Elfstrom, Denise (Pixie) (Haug), 28,
    29, 158
Elfstrom, Ginny, 158
Elfstrom, Kim (Johnson), 28, 29
Elfstrom, Larry, 28, 158
Elfstrom, Marci (Osborne), 28, 29,
    158
Elle Kari, 129
Ellis Island, 40
Erickson, Selma (Lindquist), 23, 26
Esbjornson, Robert, 124

Fairweather, Jim 158
Falk Drug Store, 14, 112
First Lutheran, St. Paul, 16, 117, 118
First Scandinavian Evangelical
    Lutheran Church, 117
First Swedish Baptist Church, 96
Flame Room, 87
Flanagan, Barbara, 133–136
Flanagan, Marie Barnes, 135
Flodquist, Carl, 130
Flodquist, Ted, 129–130
Freeman, Orville, 138
Fridley, Russell R., 138
Fridlund, Big Vic, 73–77
Fridlund, Harold, 74
Fridlund, Lindy, 73

Fridlund, Little Vic, 73–77
Fridlund, Mabel Lincoln, 74–77
Furness, Laura, 58, 60
Furness, Alexander Ramsey, 60
Furness, Anita, 60
Furness, Marion, 60–63

Gammelgården Museum, 121
Gävle, Sweden, 102
Gethsemane Lutheran, 26
Gillespie, Austin, 158
Gillespie, Jim, 158
Gillespie, Joe, 158
Gillespie, John Michael Jr. (Mike), 13,
    158
Gillespie, Renee Weberg, 128–131
glögg, 139
Golden Strings, 86–88
Göteborg, 55, 79, 93, 107
Grann, Audrey, 111
Grann, Phyllis, 111
Greupner, Jessica, 140
Gustaf VI Adolf, 71
Gustavsson, Nils, 33
Gustavus Adolphus College, 122
Gustavus Adolphus Hall, 96

Hälsa dem därhemma, 88
Hansen, Charlotte Lindquist, 17, 23
Haroldsen, Jennie Olstad, 60
Hasty Tasty Café, 95
Heimark, Dana, 61, 65
Hilding, Maureen Linnea, 96
Holmgren, Charlie, 81
Hunter, Grace, 36
Hyllengren Ruth Fardig, 123
Hyllengren, Berenice, 122
Hyllengren, William (Pastor), 119,
    121–124, 132

Ingebretsen, Charles, 146
Ingebretsen, Charles (Bud), 147
Ingebretsen, Julie, 146
Ingebretsen's, 51, 139, 143, 146–148

Jämtland, Sweden, 17
Jaros, Tony, 108
Johanesson, Albin Emanuel, 40
Johnson Harry, 15
Johnson & Berg, 27
Johnson Drug, 14
Johnson, Adolf, 27
Johnson, Albin (Uncle Al), 36–41
Johnson, Alma, 37
Johnson, Audrey Gram, 111–116
Johnson (Jonsson), Axel, 79–82
Johnson, Betty, 112
Johnson, Carl, 27
Johnson, Dr. Brad, 113
Johnson, Edith Hildeen, 79–82
Johnson, Emeroy, 118
Johnson, Gunvor, 143
Johnson, Herman, 14, 27
Johnson, Jenny, 100
Johnson, Matilda "Tillie" Nelson, 27
Johnson, Oskar, 27
Johnson, Robert R. (Bob), 79
Johnson, Ted, 83
Johnston, L.A. (Pastor), 117
julskinka, 148
Västerbotten (cheese), 148

Kalmar Castle, Småland, 81
karameller, 140
Karlsson, Gunhild Linnea, 93
Karlsson, Margit, 93
Karstadt, Bruce, 156–157
King Carl XVI Gustaf of Sweden, 93,
    94

Krefting, Emma, 23
Kristina (character in book), 149

Lake Siljan, 32, 129
Lakers, 107–109
Larson, Ida Theresa Swanson, 61
Leksand, 69
Levander, Harold, 138
Leverentz, Dave, 158
Leverentz, Steve 158
Leverentz family, 15
Lewis, Alexandra (Alix), 140
limpa, 139
Lind, Jenny, 118
Lindbloom, Hilma, 102
Lindgren, Frank, 26
Lindquist, Alice, 26
Lindquist, Charlotte, 23–26
Lindquist, Earle, 26
Lindquist, Harry, 20, 23
Lindquist, Rodger, 26
Lindquist, Ruth, 26
Lindquist, Selma Erickson, 23
Lindgren, Astrid, 56
Ljungdahl Johan Carlsson, 124
Lofgren, John, 99
Lorch Charlotte Larson, 61
Lorentzen, Ronnie, 15
Lucia Day, 49, 99, 135, 140
Lund, Sven & Ida Marie, 135
lussekatter, 141
lutefisk, 139
lutfisk, 144

MacPhail School of Music, 87, 88
Madicken, 56
Malmö, Sweden, 40

Malmquist, Rey, 71
Mary Chase, 111–112
Mattiasdotter, Elisabeth, 124
McGrath, Lorraine Wallberg, 43, 83, 102–106
Medelpad, Sweden, 96
Merchants Block, 78
Metropolitan Youth Orchestra, 88
Midsommar Dag (Midsummer Day), 103, 139
Mikan,George, 108
Mikkelsen, Vern, 108
Minneapolis Star, 133
Minneapolis Star Tribune, 133
Minnesota Historical Society, 138
Moberg, Vilhelm, 33, 149
Model Market, 146–147
Montén, A. P., 117
Moonen, Ann-Christine, 143
Mora, Minnesota, 129
Mount Olivet Careview, 127
Mount Olivet Lutheran Church, 110, 125, 127
Mount Olivet Rolling Acres, 127

Nelson, Arlett Bredesen, 14
Nelson, Carl, 14
Nelson, Christine, 14, 27
Nelson, Clarence, 125
Nelson, John, 14
Nelson, Ruth Youngdahl, 125
Neumann, Carole, 36–37
New Viking Hall, 91
Nicholson, Franz, 19
Nieland, Russ, 17, 158
Nilsson, Christina (Turnblad), 154
Nordic Roots Music Festival, 83, 157
Norelius, Eric, 117–120, 123

Northland Creamery, 37
Nybro, Småland, 79

Ohleen Dairy, 96–97
Ohman, Axel, 69–72
Ohman, Dennis Holger, 70
Ohman, Gudrun (Goody), 69–72
Olle I Skratthult, 102
Olson, Floyd B., 138
Olsson, Anders & Maria Nelsson, 129
Olsson, Andrew, 129
Olsson, Anna, 129–131
Olsson, Carin, 129
Olsson, Nels, 129, 131
Olsson, Olaf, 129–130
Osborne, Marci Elfstrom, 27, 143, 158
Oscar Danielson Orchestra, 83, 84 88, 90, 91
Oskar, Karl (character in book) 149
Osman, Linnea, 102–104
Öster, Annette, 140
Osterbauer, Karen, 143
Östlund, Elin (Blomquist), 19
Östlund, Peter, 19
Owen, Robert, 40

pepparkakor, 141
Peterson, J. Rudolph, 87
Peterson, Pete, 17
Pettit, Mildred, 73, 74
Pommer, John, 61

Ramsey House, 60, 61
Ramsey, Alexander, 58–63
Rättvik, Sweden, 32
Ready Meats, 139, 144–145
Red & White Grocery (Blomquist's), 18
Rice, John, 13,

Rip Day, 113
Robertson, Annie, 58–66
Ronning Jim, 15
Ronning Opal, 15
Rydåker Ewa Söderström, 46–51
Rydåker, Anders, 47–51
Rydåker, Louise, 48, 50
Rydåker, Sofie, 48, 50

Salem Church Dining Hall, 21
Salem Evangelical Lutheran Church,
    15,21,27, 30
Samuelson, Daisy, 100
Sandy Gus, 75
Sanford, Barbara Flanagan, 133–136
Sanford, Earl, 135
Swedlund family, 15
Seven Corners, 14
Shaft, Shirley Bjerk, 17, 158
Shaft, Big Jim, 17, 158
Shaft, Leslie 17
Shaft, Jimmy 17, 158
Sheehan, Al, 87
Shimshock, Cliff, 144
Shimshock, George, 144
Shimshock, John, 144
sillsallad, 139
Skåne, Sweden, 121, 122
Småland, 19, 23, 37, 73, 121, 154
Smålandsposten, 40
Smith, C.A., 14, 24
Snoose Boulevard, 83, 89
Soderholm, Mildred (Sody), 114
Söderström, Håkan, 46
Söderström, Svea, 46
Sollerön, Sweden, 129
South Side Auditorium, 85, 90
Sparrman, Helga, 99

spritz, 139
St. Anthony, 33,35
St. Paul Swedish Male Chorus, 104
St. Paul Swedish Men's Chorus, 83
St. Paul's Lutheran Church, 66
Stjärna, Östergötland, Sweden, 107
Storm family, 15
Svendahl, Mike, 148
Svenska Amerikanska Posten, 92–93,
    122, 151
Svenska Skolan, 49
Svenskarnas Dag, 71, 74, 103, 139,
    135
Svenskarnas Dag Girls Choir, 113
Svensson, Inga , 58–66
Svithiod Society, 95
SWEA-Minnesota, 49
Swede Hollow, 13, 61, 118, 137
Swedish Brothers Insurance, 74
Swedish Hospital , 111–116
Swedish Hospital School of Nursing,
    111–115
Swedish Nightingale, 118
Swenson, Ingrid (Inga), 61
sylta, 139, 144, 148

Thill, Polly, 74
Tiblin, Mariann, 52–54, 143
Tracie, Gordon, 105
Turnblad, Lillian, 154–155
Turnblad, Swan J., 82, 122, 151–155
Twin Cities Folk Dancers, 42
Twin City Swedish Folk Dancers, 102

Uppsala, 48

Värmland, 27–28, 122, 143
Värmländska, 29

Värmlänning, 19, 27
Vasa Children's Home, 122
Vasa Lutheran Church, 119, 153
Vasa, Minnesota, 119–121, 154
Västergötland, Sweden, 79

Walen, Jenny, 65
Wallberg, John, 33, 42–45, 83,
    102–106
Wallberg, John Per (Per Johan),
    102
Webber Park (Also Camden Park),
    17
Weberg, Martin, 130–131
Weberg, Milt, 130
Weberg, Regina (Jeannie), 131
Weberg, Ron, 131
Weberg, Ruth Chrislock, 130
White Star Lunch, 80
White Star Saloon, 78–80
Widstrand, Mrs. C.A., 33

Youngdahl, Ben, 125
Youngdahl, Carl, 125
Youngdahl, John, 124
Youngdahl, Luther, 138
Youngdahl, Luther (Governor),
    125
Youngdahl, Mabel, 125
Youngdahl, Myrtle, 125
Youngdahl, Nora, 125
Youngdahl, Oscar, 125
Youngdahl, Paul (Pastor), 126, 127
Youngdahl, Peter, 125
Youngdahl, Reuben, 125, 127

Zion Lutheran Church, 132
Zorn, Anders, 130

The Author

Anne Gillespie Lewis was born in Minneapolis and grew up in the Camden neighborhood in north Minneapolis. She studied journalism at the University of Minnesota and worked as a sports writer for the old Minneapolis Star before becoming a freelance writer.

She has written several books, including *The Minnesota Guide* (Fulcrum Publishing, 1999) and *The American Swedish Institute: Turnblad's Castle* (The American Swedish Institute, 1999).

She and her husband, Stephen, live in Minneapolis.

Anne Gillespie Lewis and Stephen Lewis met in Scandinavia and love visiting there. This photo was taken in Tampere, Finland, in August of 2001. Ilona Patajoki Photo, courtesy of Anne Gillespie Lewis.